W9-AKA-794

For Lindsay

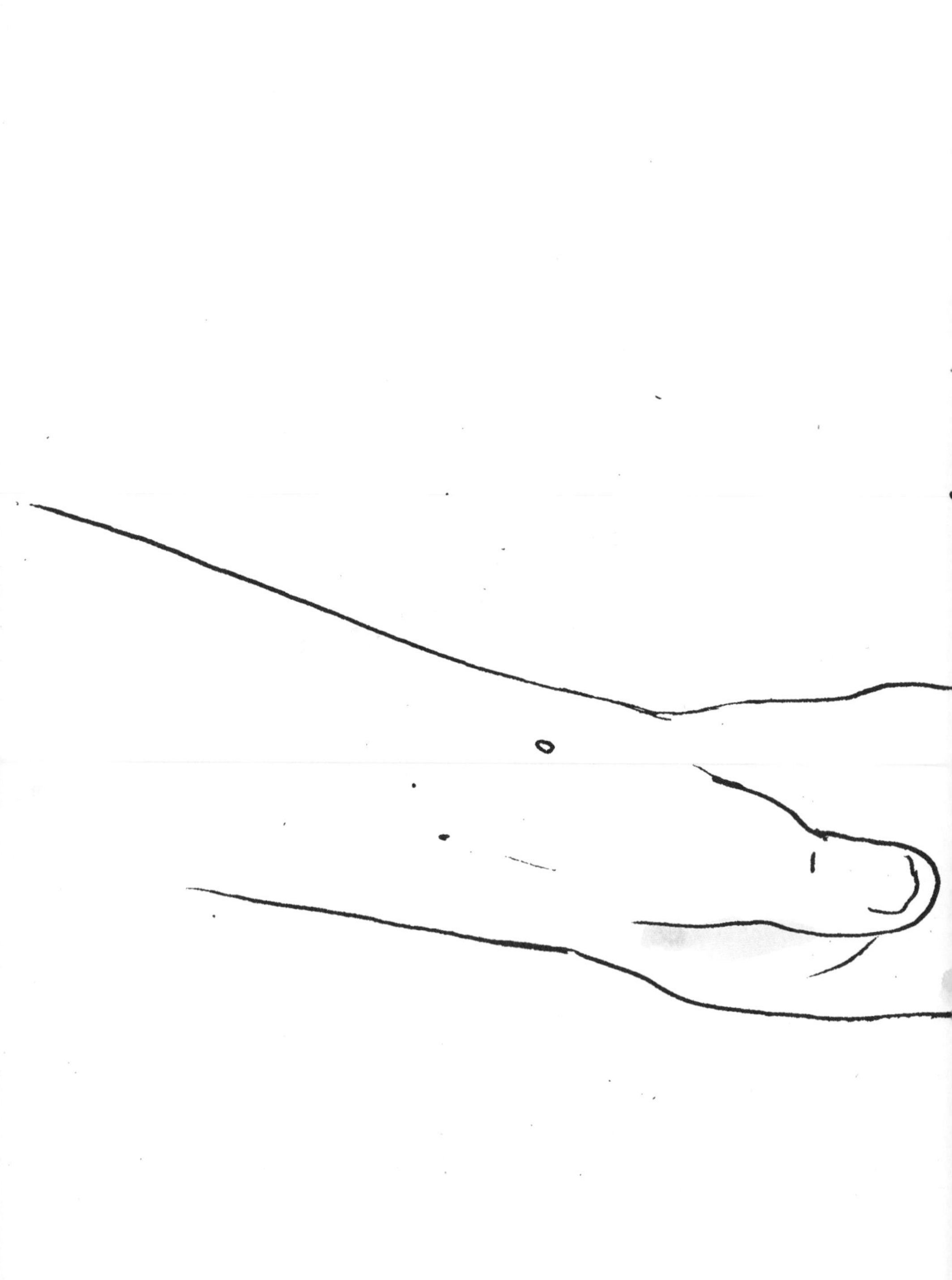

tillie walden

Spinning

:01
first second
New York

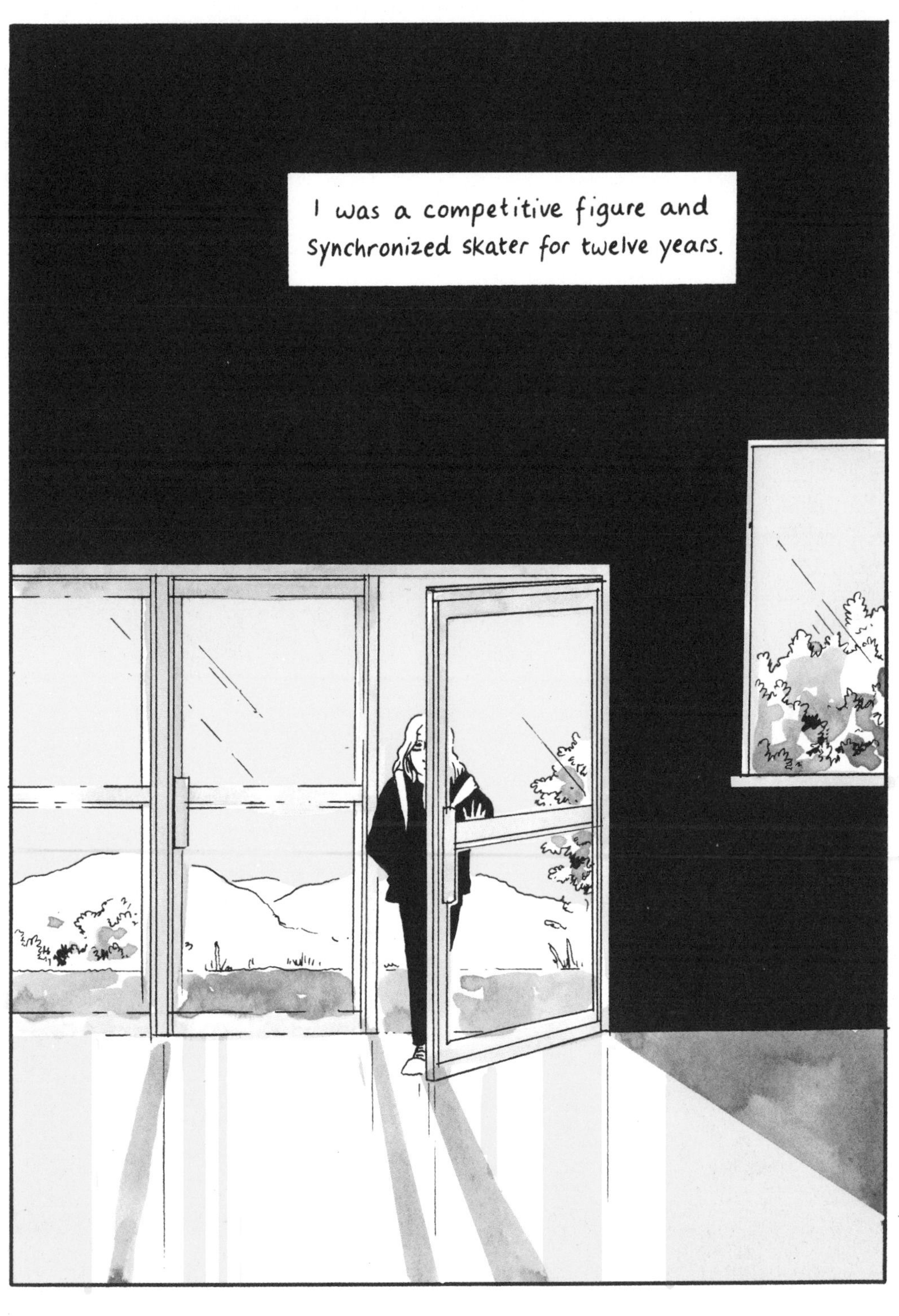
I was a competitive figure and synchronized skater for twelve years.

And as much as it makes me cringe, an ice rink will always be a familiar place.
You can get ready in locker room 2.
thanks

It smells like hockey sweat and artificial cold.
3

Every rink smells the same. They look the same, too.

Everything feels just like it used to and I want to run away.

Hey, um, do you need a hair tie?
I'm **fine**, thank you.

God, what if I fall right when I step on...

No. There's no way...

There's no way I could forget.

1

WALTZ JUMP

One of the first jumps I ever learned. I still remember the feeling of my leg swinging through and the motion throwing me into the air.

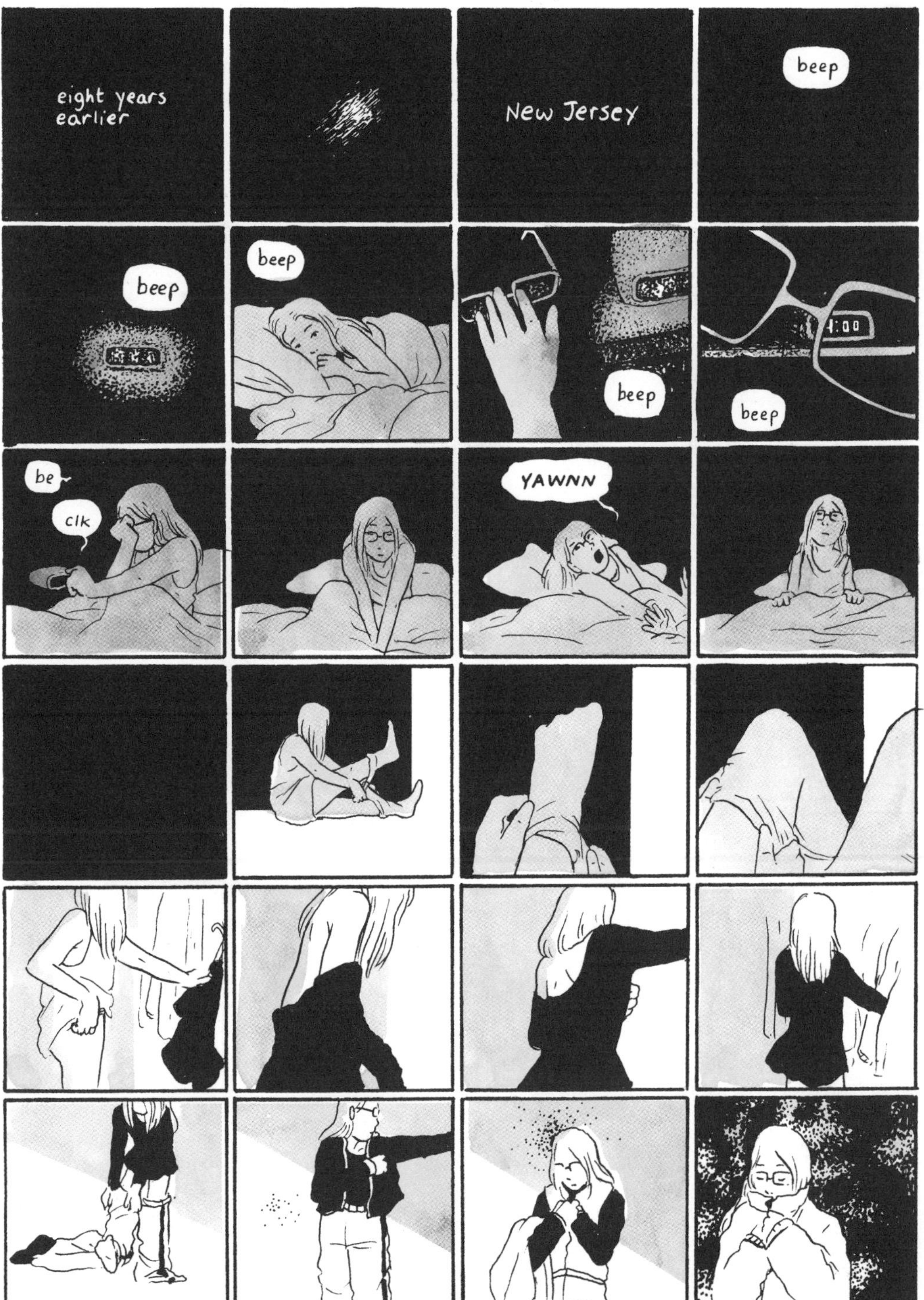
eight years
earlier
New Jersey
beep
beep
beep
beep
beep
be
clk
YAWNN

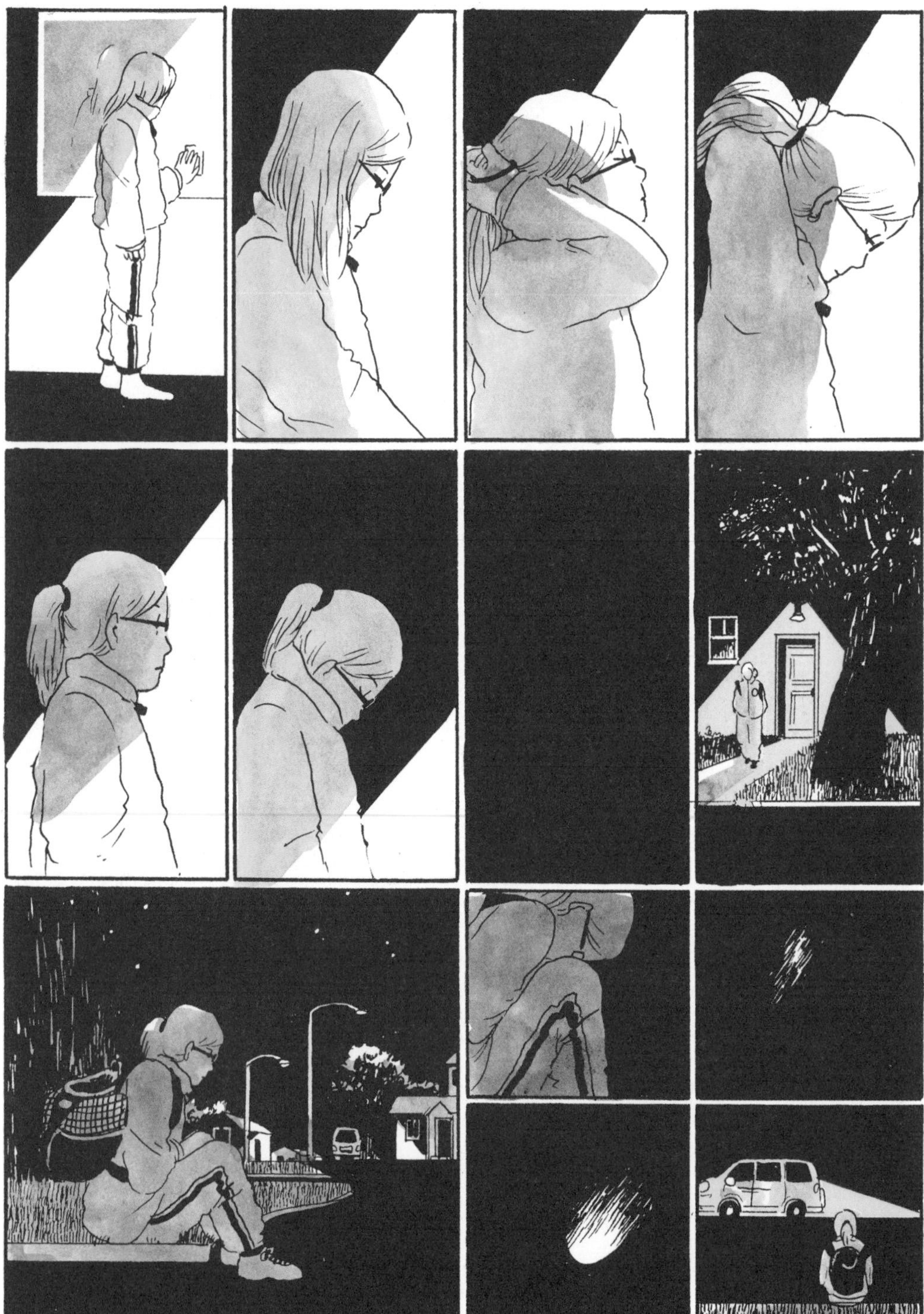

Hey, Molly.
mnnn
There's a muffin for you, Tillie.
thank you

MOLLY, use a BRUSH.
I WILL
MOLLY
OKIKNOW
GOD
Hurry UP, Molly.
You could've waited for me! Jeez.

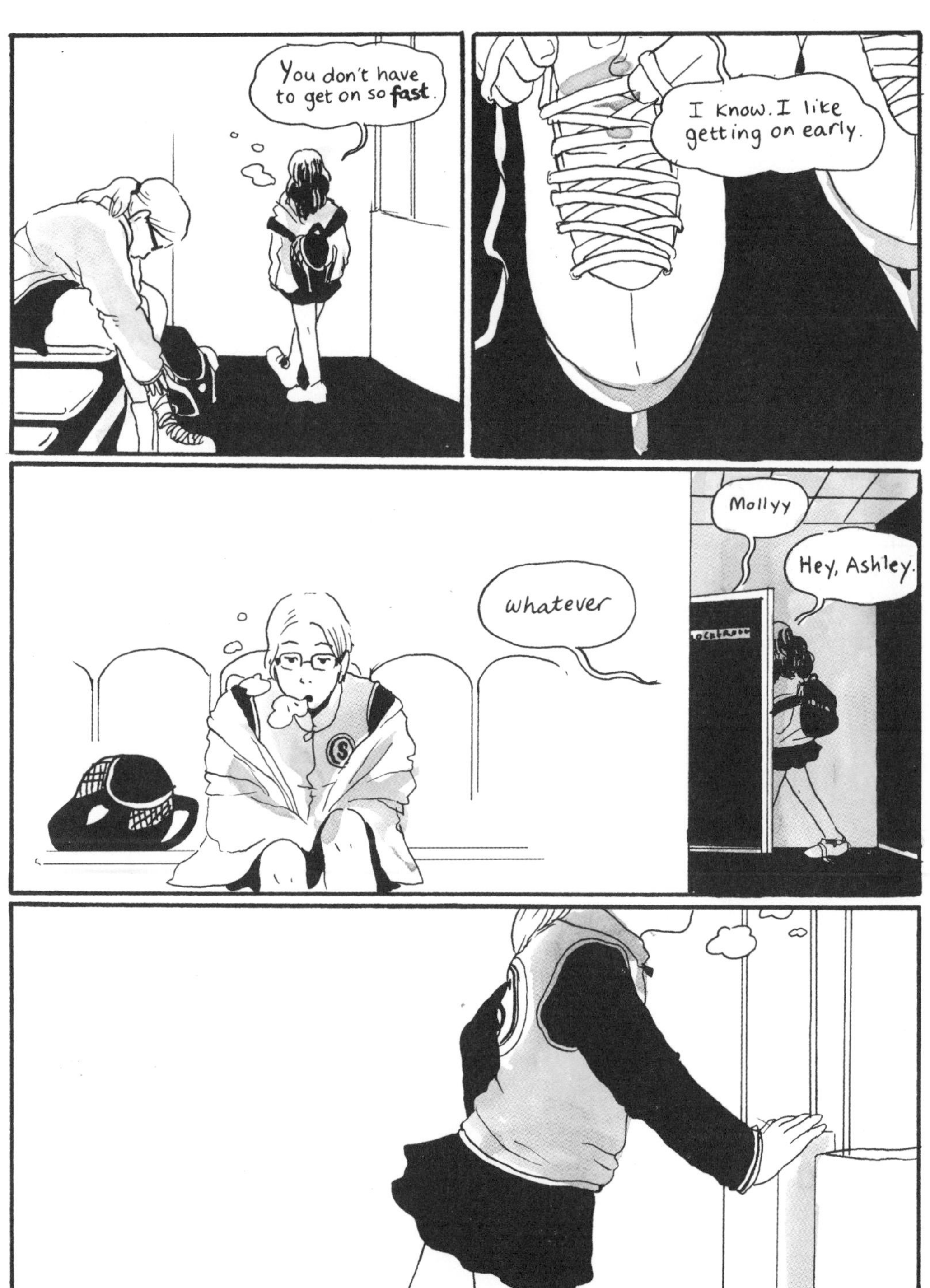
You don't have to get on so **fast**.
I know. I like getting on early.
whatever
Mollyy
Hey, Ashley.

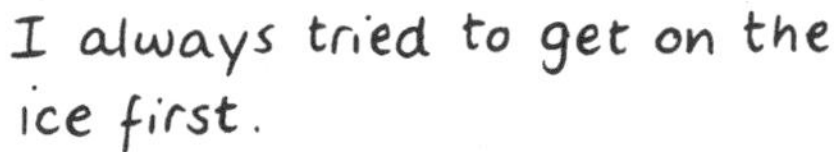
I always tried to get on the ice first.

It always felt good to be alone in such a big rink. It was all mine.

And the best part was that all the other girls were getting ready in the locker room. No one could watch me.

Once the other girls got on, our coach put on our warm-up music.

It was the same song every morning.

♪

♪ come sail away ♪

♪ come sail away, come sail away with me ♪

ALL RIGHT, GIRLS! CIRCLE UP!

The Cape Cod Classic is one week away. We'll be doing a full run-through.

I expect clean footwork, correct arms, and big smiles.

All right. PLACES!

MOVE!
Watch it, Molly!

What's with you two?
We're always like this...

Molly's always trying to be better than me. It drives me crazy.

5 6 7 8!

NO!

NO STOP NO!
NO
NO

TORI! Learn the circle footwork. UNACCEPTABLE.
Sorry
UNACCEPTABLE

And MOLLY. Your arms were all on the wrong count. FIX IT.

She looks like she's gonna cry...
who wouldn't...

Am I interrupting, ladies?

No I'm sorry.

FROM THE TOP!

Flora, you're turning too soon in the kickline.
Ashley, keep your head up.
RUN IT AGAIN.

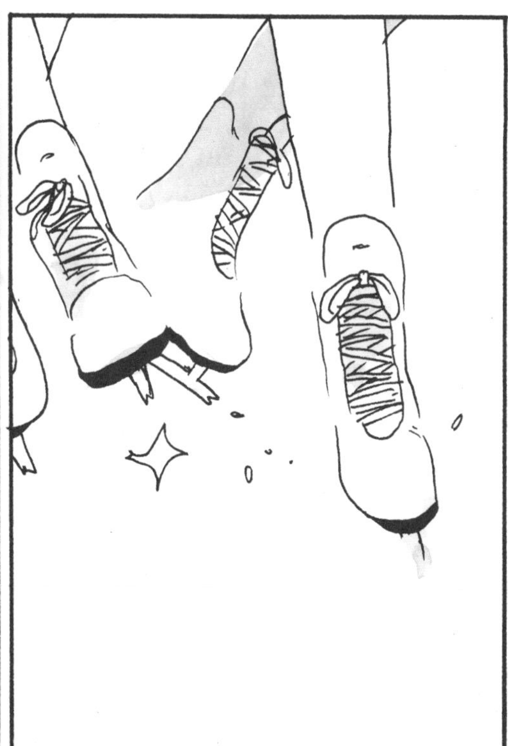

Molly!

Are you OK?
My leg. I think Jess's blade got me.

Should I...
Ask Coach if I can take Molly off the ice?

FROM THE TOP!

Ms. Joulwan, Molly hurt her leg.
I got her.

I'm FINE, you can go.

Fine, fine, I'm going.

Coming!

Hey
Hey

What're you playing?
Pokémon silver.
beep

My tights make the floor all slippery!
beep

haha
hah

Ah, crap.
What?

I forgot to finish my social studies.
You can copy mine.

No, my work is different from yours...
But we're in the same class.

Mine is special. It's why I sit with the dumb kids.
Joe! John! Tillie!

What, Mom?
beep

John, turn it off.
beep
John! Turn the game off!
well.
We're... moving. To Texas.
What?

2

SCRATCH SPIN

I always hated scratch spins.

I would get going too fast and could never figure out how to slow down.

After finishing 5th grade, we moved to Austin. Even though we waited for school to be out to leave, it still felt like it had happened too fast.

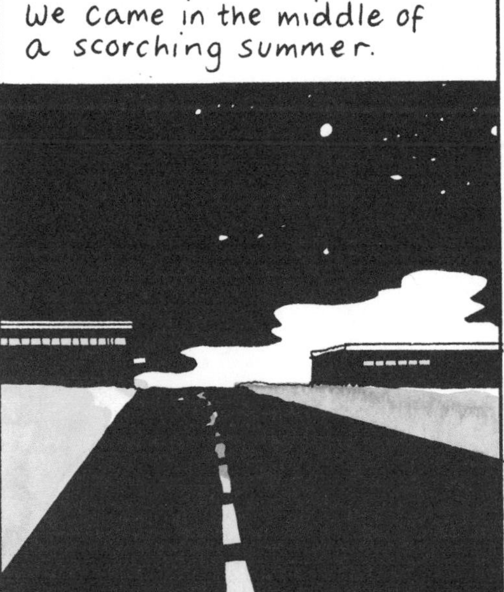

We came in the middle of a scorching summer.

On one of those hot August mornings, just a few weeks after moving in, I went to practice at my new rink.

JACK #9
* GO TROJANS! *
You awake?
yeah

Are you sure this is it?
well - no.

DAD
It's OK, I think this is it.

What percentage?

What?

What percentage do you think this is it?
mmm
DAD
Fine, fine. 70%.

That's not enough.

It's locked - let's leave.
No - I see girls inside - HELLO?
Dad, wait
HI! IS THIS THE RINK?
Oh - HAHA, thanks - it's the other door.
T? You coming?
Yeah.

None of the girls spoke to me that day. But with careful listening I figured out their names.

Michaela.

Jennifer.

Rosalind.

Dasha, and her
sister, who I
called "little Dasha."

All right, Till. I'll leave you to it.
Have a good skate.

Are you Tillie?

Your mom told you about me, right? I'm Caitlin, your new coach.

Ready to get on the ice?
Okay.

So... do you want to warm up?
okay.

They didn't even know my name yet, but they had to see if I was a threat.

I was.

Want to start with some jumps? I'm still working out your level.

How'd it go, T?

Fine. Let's go.

Hey.
hmm

Want to stop for coffee? Maybe a scone?

Not only was skating different here, school was something else entirely.

After facing relentless bullying and getting terrible grades at my public school back in New Jersey, my parents decided to send me to private school, hoping I would fare better.

PURNELL
SCHOOL

What class?
What?
Oh-6th grade math, I think.

Follow me.

I'm Ms. Ramberg. I'll be teaching your English class later today.

Hey-who're you?
Tillie
You're new?

yes
WAIT
What?

I love your name. I'm Rae, by the way.
Rae.

It always frustrated me how easily a girl could make me dizzy.
New girl!

I just moved here... from New Jersey.
NEW JERSEY?

Wow, I can't hear your accent at all.

My days were long. The mornings were filled with figure skating practices...
and my afternoons belonged to synchronized skating.
We need to leave.
I KNOW.
Hello, Cloudy.
mrow
This new jacket is weird, clouds.
You'll never get used to it.
prrr
TILLIE
I gotta go, cloudy.

Mom, this is a mall.

How're we gonna practice in a mall?

This was where Caitlin said the rink was.
excuse me

POP!
MOM, wait- don't bother them-
excuse me

Why isn't synchro at the rink I go to in the mornings?!
I don't know!

See? I think that's your team down there.

wait

Go down there! Tillie - Jesus Christ, don't cry.

I felt like I was going to hurl.
woahh

No WAY, carly.
haha
She did! She ate it!

I had hoped some of the girls from my morning practice would be here, but no one was familiar.
Hi-um, I'm Tillie.
Who?
oh yeah...

My mom said I had to show you around.

I'm Carly.
Oh, hi.

COME ON!
Oh! Sorry!

I'm Trinity. This is Taylor.
Trinity, shut up. I can tell her myself.
I'm Sarah.
GUYS! Hurry up, I want a pretzel.
I always hated meeting new people. I never knew what to say...
cool... cool names...

So, like, you can hang out with the girls on our team, the Sparkling Stars, but, like, the older girls are off-limits.
50%

Older girls?
The teenager team. The Austintatious Stars...

Yeah, um-
over there

Oh my gosh
COME ON.

Once I got a glimpse of the older team, I knew that was where I wanted to be.
Sorry

Tillie - have you read Twilight?
Twilight?

of course
omg
us too
Edward or Jacob?
OBVIOUSLY Edward.
omg Tillie. Yes

GIRLS!
um
lol

Is practice starting?
no way
GIRLS

GIRLS! Let's go! Block formation!

LINE UP!
duhh

Hey! Quit squeezing my arm!
whoa

All right, girls - TAYLOR, please focus.

TAYLOR!
In New Jersey, the discipline and tension of practice had terrified me.

But I found myself missing it. The screaming, the crying, the exhaustion. It seemed so far away now.
OKAY! 5678!

I had hoped that the simple familiarity of synchro would make me feel comfortable here.

But even that didn't work out as planned.
OK, ladies, let's run the splice.

I quickly found out that skating here operated on an entirely different system than the one back in New Jersey.
"splice?"

Formations had different names, levels and titles changed, even judging was different.
What's a splice?!

The one part of my life that I thought I understood was plunged into confusion with everything else.
uh... the two line... mix together thing?

OH. You mean an intersection?
A what?

While synchro remained baffling, my early morning private lessons weren't too hard to get through.
Morning, Caitlin.
Morning.

So, what were your lessons like in New Jersey?

um
well

What were you and your coach working on?

I was lucky to get Caitlin as a coach.
Hmm, footwork, jumps, spins...

Just normal stuff, I guess.
She wasn't nearly as strict as some of my past coaches. She never yelled at me, she never made me jump endlessly or skate until I was sick.

But I had also had coaches who had loved me and cared about me.

I never felt that from Caitlin.

But in the beginning it felt ok to give that up for Caitlin's neutrality.

Bring your arms down a little.

You don't have to hold them so high.

After training with Caitlin for a few months, I took my first Texas test at a scrubby rink in Dallas.

DR PEPPER STAR CENTER OF DALLAS

Testing determined my group at competition. It was also an experience a skater always went through with their coach. My first test with Caitlin felt like a milestone. She was by my side now, and memories of old coaches no longer had a place.

Do it like we practiced and you'll pass with flying colors.
Right.

You'll be testing pre-Juv today, correct?
yes.

You may begin.

I tested about once a year and always passed.

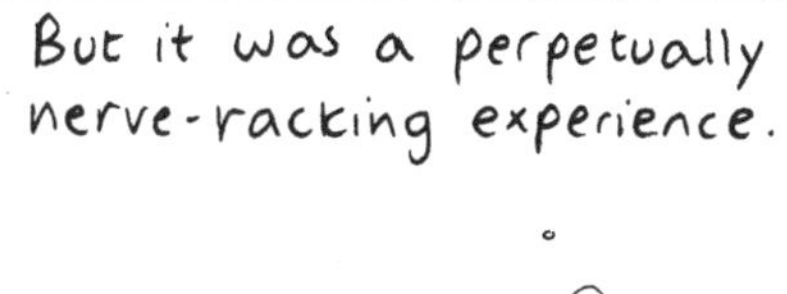
But it was a perpetually nerve-racking experience.

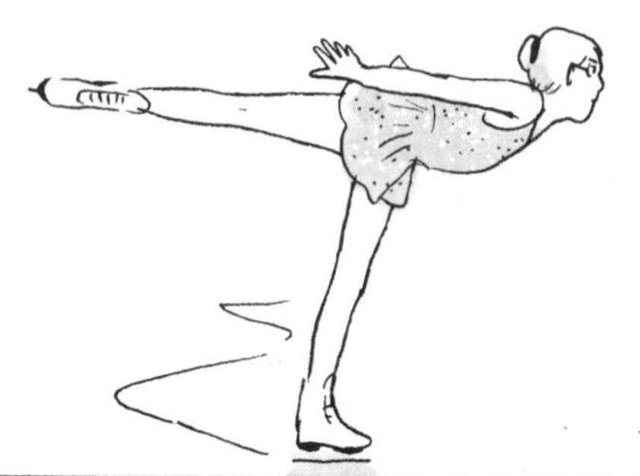
No music was allowed. The only sound in the whole rink was my blades scraping the ice.

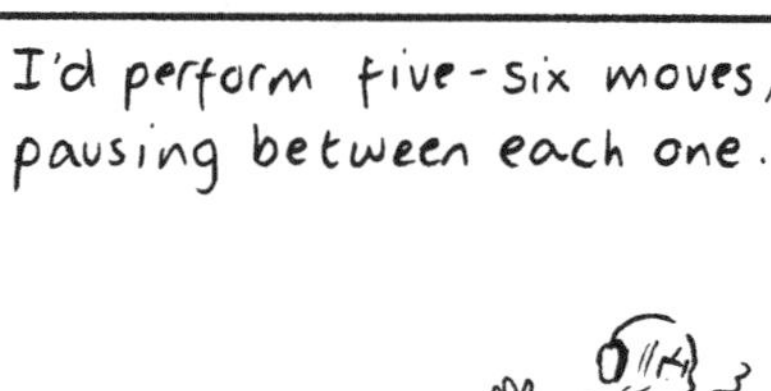
I'd perform five-six moves, pausing between each one.

The pauses killed me. Silence would fill the rink.

The judges would have their heads down, scribbling their comments.

My coach, blurry and far away.

I'd feel my lungs swallowing frigid air, trying to keep up,

and my face and arms would prickle with cold sweat.

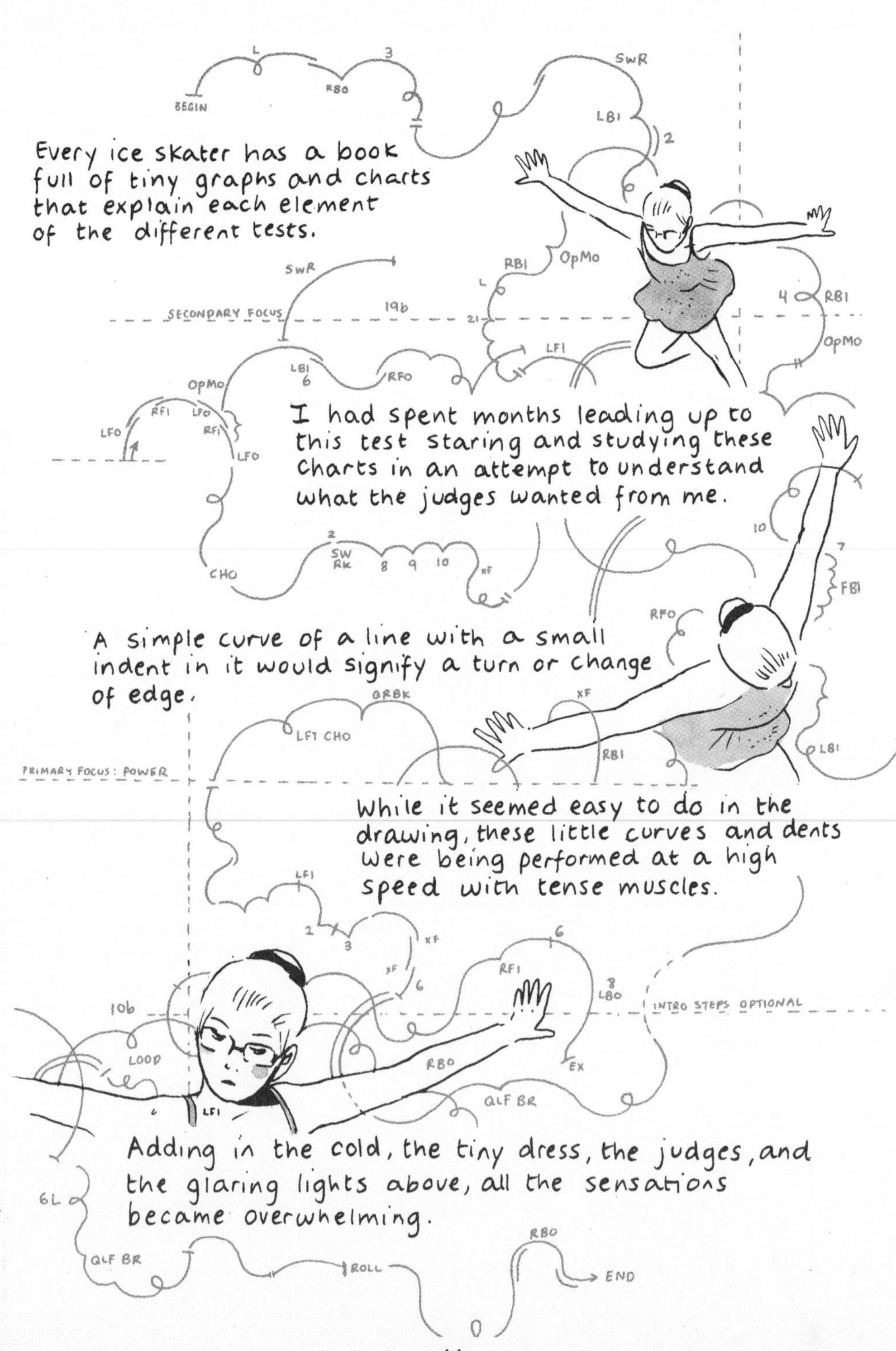
BEGIN
L
RBO
3
SwR
LBI
2
Every ice skater has a book full of tiny graphs and charts that explain each element of the different tests.
SwR
RBI
OpMo
L
SECONDARY FOCUS
19b
21
4
RBI
OpMo
LFI
LBI
6
RFO
OpMo
RFI
LFO
RFI
LFO
LFO
I had spent months leading up to this test staring and studying these charts in an attempt to understand what the judges wanted from me.
10
7
FBI
2
SW
RK
8
9
10
XF
CHO
RFO
A simple curve of a line with a small indent in it would signify a turn or change of edge.
QRBK
LFT CHO
XF
RBI
LBI
PRIMARY FOCUS: POWER
While it seemed easy to do in the drawing, these little curves and dents were being performed at a high speed with tense muscles.
LFI
2
3
XF
XF
6
6
RFI
8
LBO
INTRO STEPS OPTIONAL
10b
LOOD
RBO
EX
QLF BR
LFI
Adding in the cold, the tiny dress, the judges, and the glaring lights above, all the sensations became overwhelming.
6L
RBO
QLF BR
ROLL
END

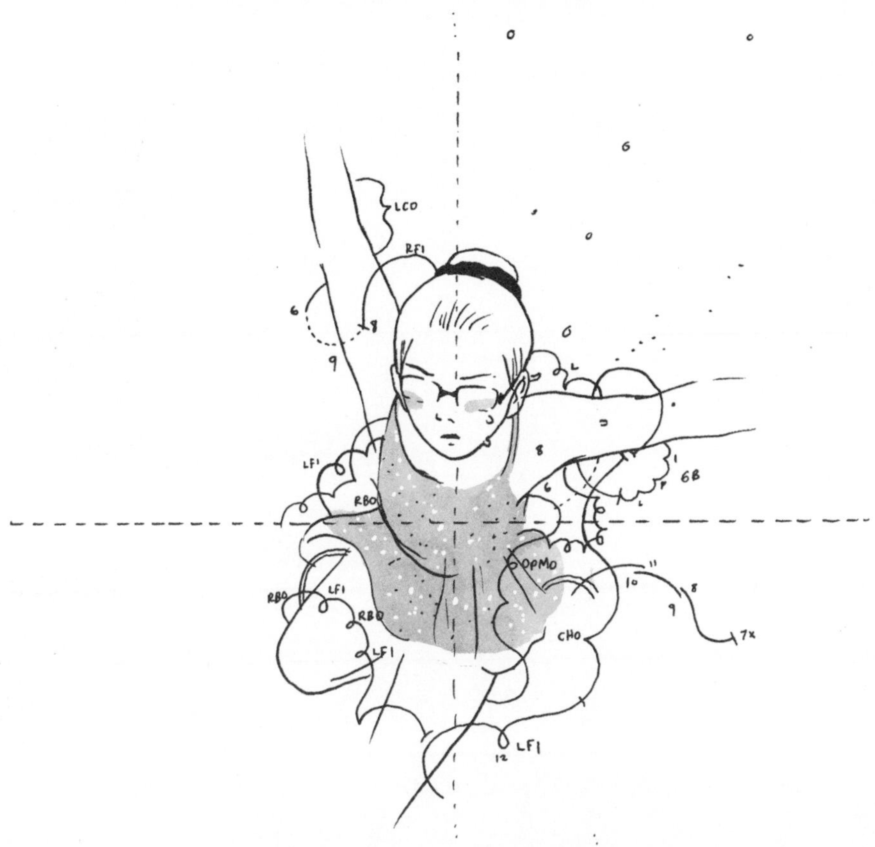

Testing felt like a prolonged spasm. My muscles were trying to recreate perfect shapes and angles while my mind churned through images and memories of the moves.

But that was how it felt. To me, that was ice skating. It wasn't large jumps or sweeping glides. It was intricate patterns and minute details under the veil of makeup and freezing air.

Thank you, Tillie.

When it was finally over, I would retreat to my jacket.

And even though I always thought I screwed up...

I kept passing.
PRE-JUVENILE
FAIL
PASS

You headed home?

Gonna watch the other testers first.
See you Friday.

The other girls always seemed so much more confident, so much more grown-up.

I never ignored the fact that I was attracted to them. I had known I was gay since I was 5. Now I was almost 12.

A teacher's aide had shown me how to hold your sleeve when you put your jacket on. I still remember her hands on my shoulders. I didn't have a word to describe it yet, but in that moment I knew.

Skating presented a strange debacle. I disliked the femininity of it all yet was attracted to it nonetheless.

I always tried not to stare too much, but -

Hey, T.

You're EARLY.

But knowing for so long still didn't make it easy.
Congrats on passing.

I knew it wasn't right and I didn't tell anyone what I felt.
eh

So I quietly fell in love, over and over again, never once thinking it could ever be real.
I always pass.

3

FLIP JUMP

I loved flips. You would launch yourself into the air by slamming the tip of your blade into the ice.

I found a routine after over half a year in Texas.
Higher, Tillie!

The other girls watched me less, accepting me as part of the scenery.

I made friends at school that helped fill the time.

And I found out quickly that a fancier school did not mean fewer bullies.

I even melded with my new synchro team, learning how they joked and how to laugh with them.

Nothing felt easy, but at least it wasn't new anymore.

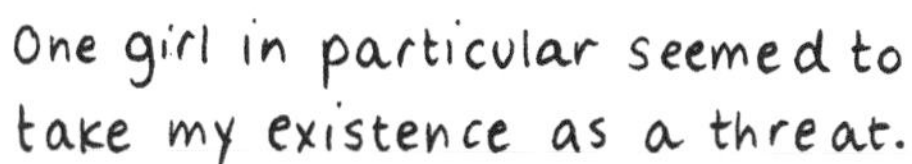

One girl in particular seemed to take my existence as a threat.

Grace.
CRACK

She was vicious to everyone, and in a tiny school there was no escape.

You okay?

RAE! Pass the ball!
Hey...

RAE
I'm fine.
OK, OK!

Seriously, it's nothing. I was in her way...
Jeez

RAE, come on!
CHILL

Go play. I'm good.

BACK IN!
yuhh

Dad, we have to leave in three minutes.
You want to eat something?
All food is disgusting.
You know, getting up at four am is tough on your pops, too.
I knoww.
I'm going to sleep for one minute.

I felt so grimy. Showers were last on my list of things I cared about.

Ice skaters were supposed to be sparkling princesses.

But princesses probably took showers.

Dad, we gotta go.

After a brutal morning practice and a long day at school, an evening practice with the Sparkling Stars did not seem worth the energy.
50%
MACES

There are three kids in my class named Braden and they ALL SUCK...
NO WAY, Braden P. is cool.
GUYS! LOOK!

You go to the same school?
GUYS!

Me'n Taylor do.
it sucks
WhatEVER, Taylor.

Look, Tillie!
cool
TRINITY, please stop.

elevation

And I was like, no thanks, dickhead
that's a SWEAR

IS NOT, SARAH.
is too
wow dude
Would you say it to your MOM?

You smell terrible.
Oh. Haha.

Hey, Sarah.

Carly was our synchro coach's daughter.
I'm a brunette now, see?

Coaches' daughters always got away with a lot.
oh my GOD.

I was only kidding! I KNOW I'm blonde, Carly.

I got... 36.
Nice, me too.

Hey, Gabi?
mmm?

What's the deal with Grace? Why doesn't she like me?

She does that to everybody.

But she wrote about ME in the bathroom, no one else!

It's probably just 'cause you're new.
Really?
Yeah.

I've known her since 2nd grade. She's always been like this.

In 4th grade she just randomly punched me.
GOD

She said an alarm went off and it just made her jump.

She convinced everyone it was an accident.

Morning,
Tillie.

Rosalind wasn't a synchro skater, so I only ever saw her at my early morning practices.

She was the only one in the rink who smiled at me.

She was 17. But I didn't care that we were 5 years apart.

She was so pretty.

She was tall.

She made those long, cold mornings just a little more bearable.

Morning, Rosalind.

Morning practices felt like a dream. I spent them watching Rosalind and running out the clock.

By contrast, synchro practices felt like my eyes had been stretched open. The mall was loud and bright, and I was perpetually trapped in the middle of my team of girls.

It came out my nose.
Do it again, Tillie.

Like this?

Your eyes, like, get **BIG**.
HAHA
HAHA

haha
ok

My cousin can do the same thing.
Let's do never have I ever.

What's that?
omg, Tillie
Hold out ten fingers.
'kay

ONOTOP
♪never have I ever♪
met a homo!
haha
good one
haha WHAT EVEN
NO-Tillie, don't put a finger down yet.
omg
haha
That means you **have** met one.
oh-
OKAYY next please
♪never have I ever♪

ANGIO'S
DEALS
That game rocks!

HEY
me?

Yeah- c'mere.

25%
What's your name?
You're the kid from New Jersey, right?

oh.OK
You can sit.
Yeah, Jesus Christ, it's not an interview.

I'm Lindsay.
Tillie.

So were you, like, Jersey Shore?

what?
Like the show.
Oh-well. I don't know.

Want some fries?
yes

I thought I was just moving up the skating social ladder by sitting with these girls. I never thought much would come of it.

But it was at that greasy table that I met Lindsay. In New Jersey, Molly had been my loyal companion. And now in Texas I had finally found someone who could fill that role.

"Always the same, but different eh? Every age, every time."

When Ms. Ramberg read aloud to us, it was the only time in school I felt perfectly at ease.
"Day was always over."

I didn't know why reading was so hard for me.
"Night was always coming."

So to hear a story with such ease was like magic.
"And aren't you always afraid, Apeman there? Or you, Mummy, that the sun will never rise again?

"Summer fell dead. Winter put it in the grave. A billion voices wept. The wind of time shook the vast house."

6th grade ended quietly and summer took over again. Even though there were still practices and competitions, I found moments of free time.
CATCH IT, JOHN!
I WILL
GET IT!
AGH!
haha
Hey-who is that?
Dunno, let's keep playing.

aw you missed
John, he's watching me...
Is he? So?
No, he's... **looking** at me.
we have to go

You have everything?
yep

Call when you get there.
I will.

yo
Hey

Hey, Tillie
Hey, Judy

You girls buckle in, I'm responsible for more than just you now, Linds.
Mom...

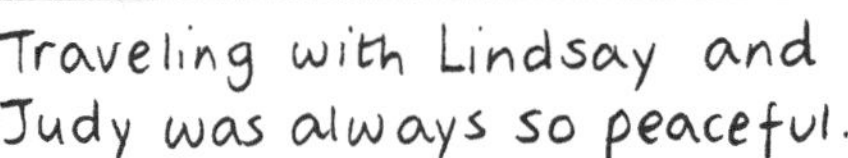
Traveling with Lindsay and Judy was always so peaceful.

They seemed so relaxed with one another, whereas I always felt so tense with my mom.
So are your parents, like, super busy?
I guess

I can record your programs on my cell phone for them to watch.
Nah it's cool...

I brought a video camera!
No, really, it's fine.

I always wanted to feel like I didn't care that my parents rarely made an appearance at competitions.

But I felt *something*. It wasn't sadness, more like embarrassment.
We're in 203.
256.

I was always the only girl in the locker room without a mom, the only one who didn't have family members lurking around the results area.

So I made Lindsay my family.

Skating was too big a world to tackle alone. So I stuck to her side, terrified of letting go.

We're only two years apart, though.

And I'm stuck with Carly and her gang.

They probably just want to keep you on the Sparkling Stars to make them better.

ugh

See you on the other side, Linds.
Good luck!

ALL RIGHT, GIRLS! Kickline order!

They better say our cheer loud.
Show the Houston All-Stars who's the best.

SO SPARKLING
All right, ladies-on three!
GO GIRLZ

SMILE

SHAKE IT

NE LOVE YOU

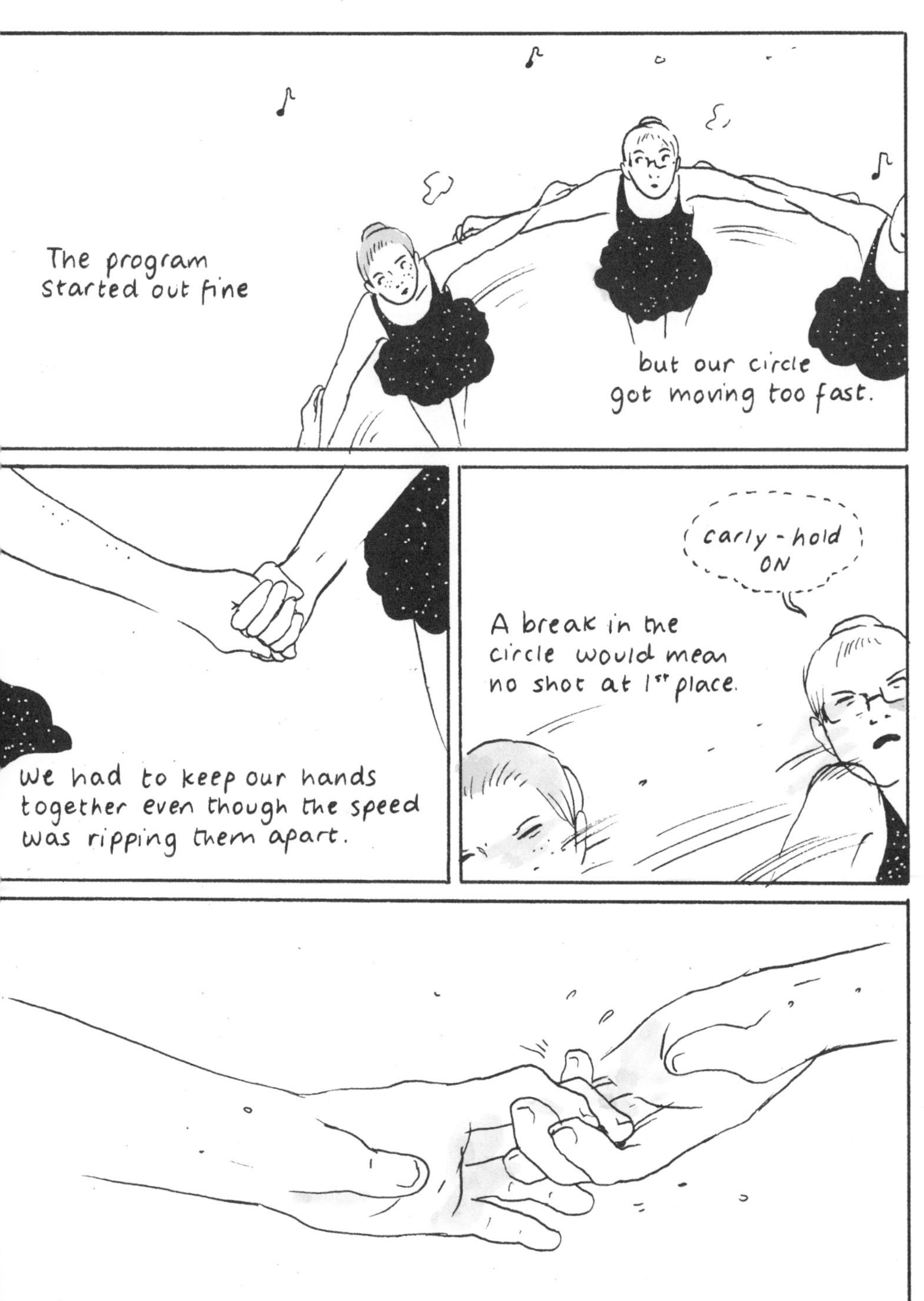
The program started out fine
but our circle got moving too fast.
We had to keep our hands together even though the speed was ripping them apart.
A break in the circle would mean no shot at 1st place.
carly - hold ON

But we made it.
And 1st place goes to...
the SPARKLING STARS!

Hey, Lindsay. Heard y'all got second.
Yeah, Dawn tripped. Congrats on the win.
thanks

What else do you have today?
Compulsories, a trio with Carly and Trinity...
yikes

We're skating to Katy Perry and I'm not about it.
You **don't** like Katy Perry?
Yikes.

Every competition for me consisted of many different programs—
And my gold is at eight pm tonight! I'm so dead!
jeez

Some synchro, some solo, some easy, some hard.
I've got ribbon in an hour and my duo tomorrow morning.
damn

My strongest events were the most technical ones, like footwork and compulsories.
Guh, I need to get ready.

Lindsay was my polar opposite. She was good at the graceful types of programs.
Let's go to the locker room.

My gold routine was my most difficult program, chock full of jumps and spins.

I was always so tense in the hours leading up to it.

At the height of my nerves, right as I was stepping onto the ice, my team would scream our chant to wish me luck.

SMILE
SHAKE IT
WE LOVE YOU

I know it was meant to be motivational, but it just left me feeling sick.

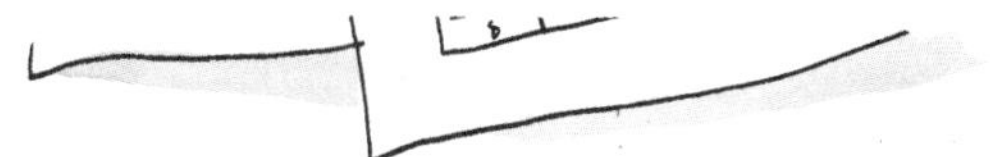

But that experience wasn't unique. Every competition was like the last, following the same rhythm.

It always started on a Friday, when a peppy rink employee would hand you a competitor's gift bag, complete with stale candy and skating-themed objects.

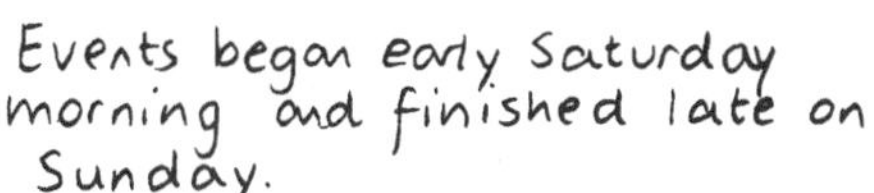

Events began early Saturday morning and finished late on Sunday.

The weekend would be filled with running and waiting. Running to change your dress after finding out your event was running early, running to find your coach or a schedule or the right lipstick.

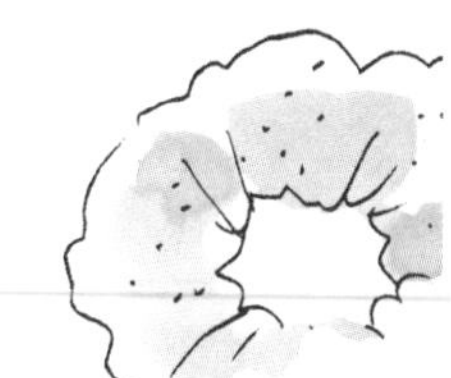

And waiting. Waiting hours between events, waiting for someone to do your hair, waiting on results.

Competitions somehow managed to be frantic and boring at the same time.
GOLD 8PM LB
1. TILLIE WALDEN FSH
2. KIERA WHALEN FSDA
3. SARINA ISRAEL DSS
4. JARAD GREENE LSC

But a win would throw the whole weekend in a new light.

How'd you do?
You'll never believe it, Judy. I got 1st!

Great job!
Lindsay...

She didn't do as well as she wanted to on her ribbon.
it was AWFUL

The other girls in your group sucked, you should've won.
they were fine...

No, they were literal monsters. One of them gave a judge a soda. That is bribery.

Come on, girls, let's get some food. Y'all must be exhausted.

Hey... Lindsay...

I'M GONNA BEAT YOU TO THE CAR!
Hey! No fair, you got a head start!

4

AXEL

I have never known a more frustrating jump.

I remember going into it, gliding backwards and holding my breath.

As I would turn to go into it I would wish and hope with everything I had that this time it would work.

But I did make a few friends. I started getting invited to sleepovers and birthday parties.

well

I'll get right to it. I've noticed you having trouble with some of the other girls.

Specifically, Grace.

It seems like there's something going on between you two. Can you tell me about it?

I wanted to tell her everything.
Grace?

About her holding me down, her writing on the mirror, her blows, her comments...

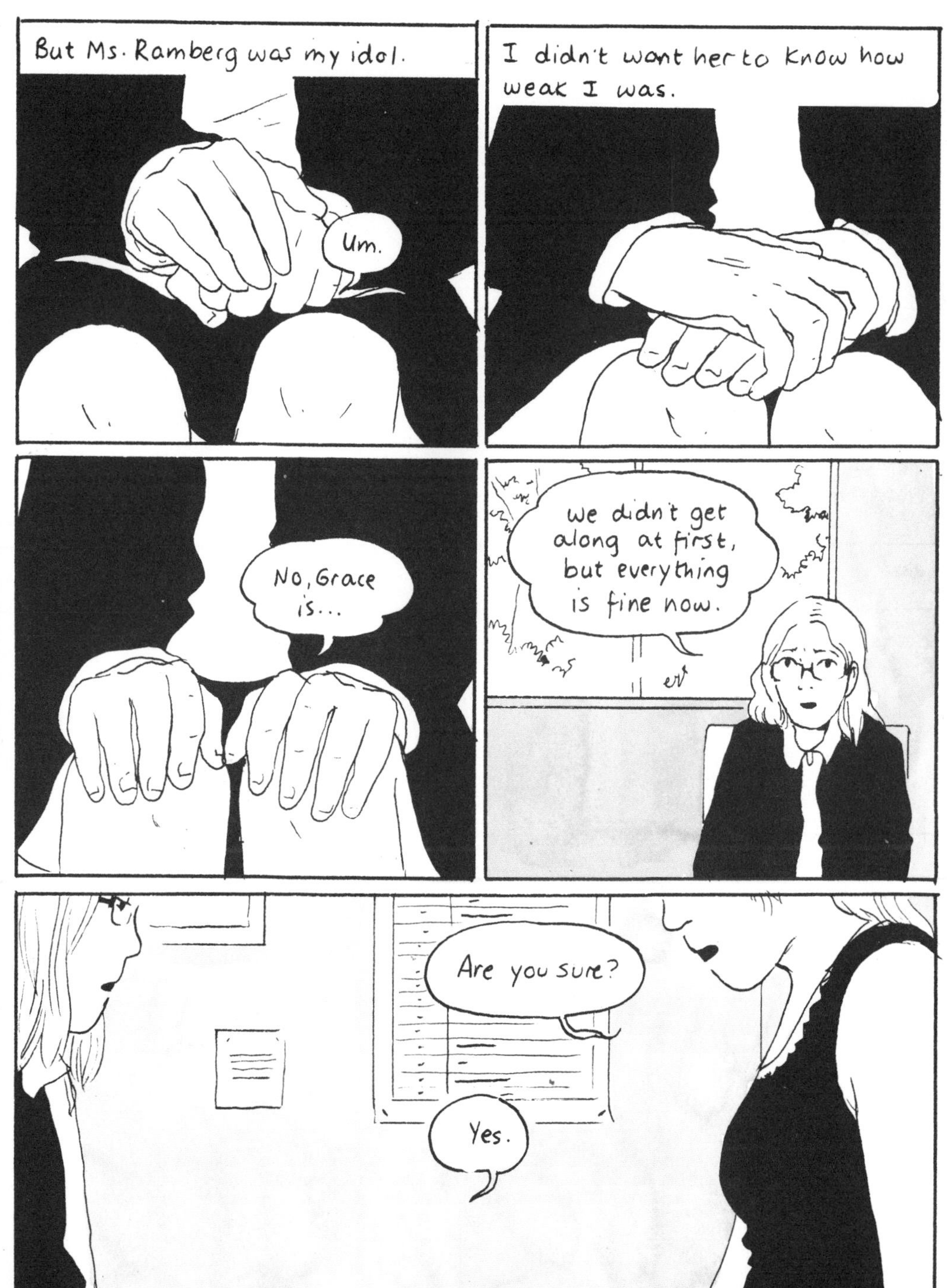
But Ms. Ramberg was my idol.
Um.
I didn't want her to know how weak I was.
No, Grace is...
we didn't get along at first, but everything is fine now.
Are you sure?
Yes.

Occasionally Lindsay and I would land on the same early morning session.

She made everything so much warmer.
morning
hey

Talking to her was so easy because I didn't have to be afraid she'd make fun of me.
brrr

She was the kindest person I'd ever met.
How are you?

OK. Rather be here than home.
Yeah?

My dad's cool, it's fun being with him.

My mom just gets mad all the time, so I stay out of her way.

Me and my twin brother are close. He's like my best friend. I never see my older brother. He dyed his hair black.

What about you?
It's just me and my mom.

Oh.
No, it's cool.

I'm used to it.

Screw this.

John-you awake?

what're you watching?
Zoey 101.
Is this season one?
Yeah, "Defending Dustin."
classic
absolutely

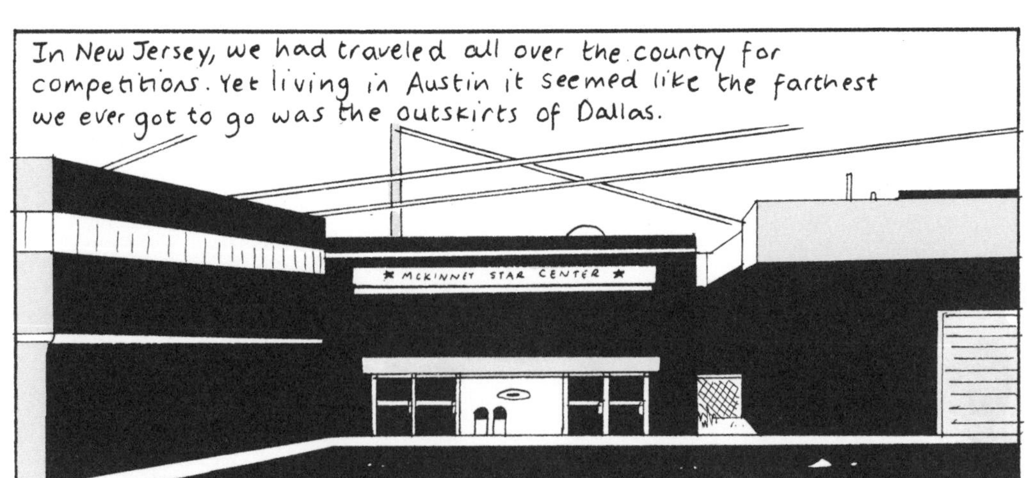
In New Jersey, we had traveled all over the country for competitions. Yet living in Austin it seemed like the farthest we ever got to go was the outskirts of Dallas.
MCKINNEY STAR CENTER

Have you guys seen Caitlin?
Locker room B.

thanks

Hold still, Tillie.

You're all set. Do your makeup then get your skates on.
'Kay
NEXT
Hey, Linds... wanna do my makeup?

Close your eyes.
'Kay

nnnooOh STOP
come on

IT'S IN MY EYES
OK
calm down

exhale

Hold still.

NGHH NO STOP PLEASE STOPPP
We still have to do mascara.

Give it
what

Your phone. Your parents will want to see.

It's in the pocket!
Good luck!

SMILE
SHAKE IT
WE LOVE YOU!

The performance always seemed blurry afterward. Watching a recording was the only way I could try to understand what had happened.

Hey.

Your results are up.

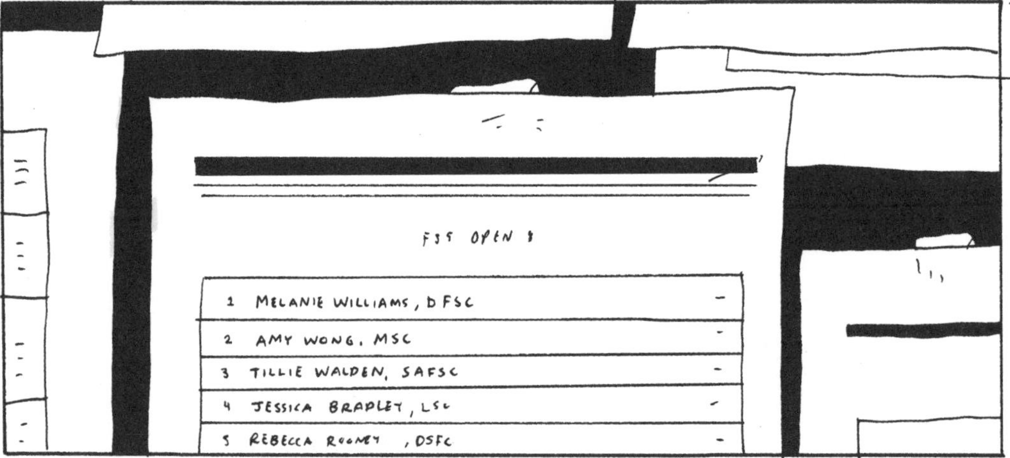
1 MELANIE WILLIAMS, DFSC
2 AMY WONG, MSC
3 TILLIE WALDEN, SAFSC
4 JESSICA BRADLEY, LSC
5 REBECCA ROONEY, DSFC

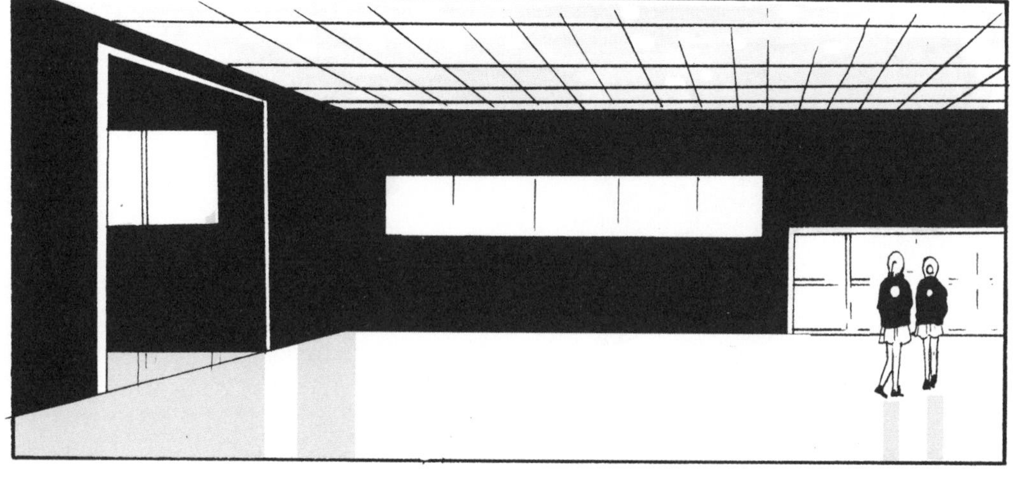

AME'S

In a way, being back at the mall was comforting after a competition.

it's true!

no way

The sounds of shoppers and the smell of perfumes and pretzels had started to become familiar.

Your old rink had DDR?
oh yeah

Well they had just remodeled the whole rink.

And the new one was like, state of the art. Arcade and all.

wow

New Jersey sounds, like, so olympic.

Haha, yeah. I guess.

You skate differently than other girls here.
I do?
Yeah, it's...
It's not, like, a bad thing, just different.
Do you miss it?
sometimes.

I miss how big the ice felt. And there was this giant window...

and there was a ballet studio INSIDE the rink! We went every Saturday.

Plus we got to travel... and, I dunno. It was just... better.

It sounds GREAT.

I didn't mean-
My practice starts soon.

feelin' out of it?

It hadn't hit me until then how long I'd been away. Over a year. Everyone in New Jersey had probably forgotten me at this point.

I missed Molly and I didn't understand why. We were constantly bickering and driving each other crazy. But I missed it. I missed being in that beautiful rink with her.

I hadn't forgotten the brutality of practices there, and I didn't miss getting yelled at. But there was something wonderful about it all. That feeling of freedom when practice was done and romping around the rink like we owned the place.

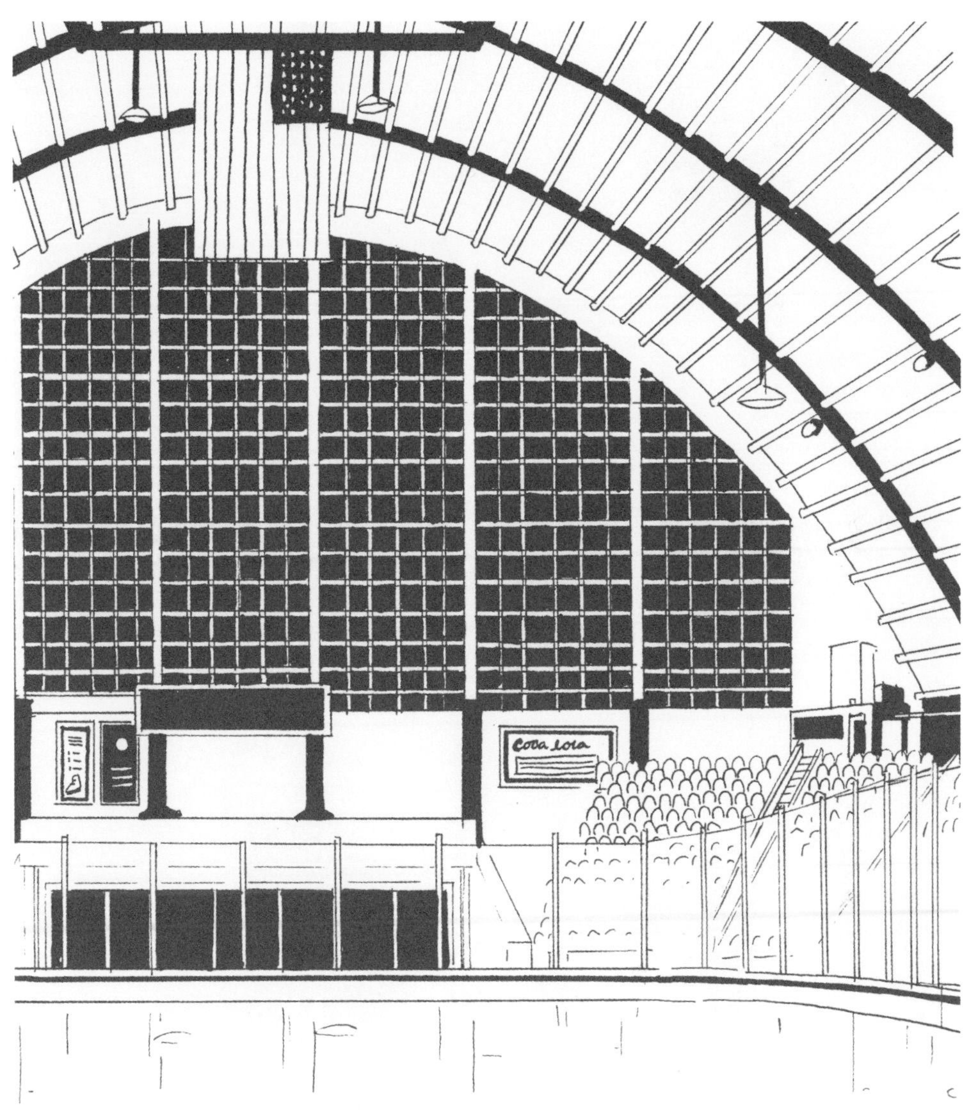

Skating changed when I came to Texas. It wasn't strict or beautiful or energizing anymore. Now it just felt dull and exhausting. I couldn't understand why I should keep skating after it lost all its shine.

But I kept going through the motions.

Willing myself to keep going, keep moving forward.

All the while keeping my eye out for any way to escape it all.

good job

1 MAY KASAHARA
2 TILLIE WALDEN
3 VIN VENTURE
4 ELLEN SCARBOROUGH
I just had to keep going.
MOM, I GOT 1st!
2nd
Great!
I guess
Next time I'll get 1st.

I had to believe that
if I kept going things
would get better.

They had to.

Didn't they?

It was when I hit the floor that I
noticed someone sitting in the corner of the room.

Each student had been assigned an older girl to help them out and be their "guide" in school.

My 8th grader was sitting in that corner.

And she didn't even look at me.

I'll never forget that carton of orange juice she was holding.

I couldn't separate school and skating anymore.

Bring your leg through!

It was all just too much.

shit

Caitlin, I need to get off.

OK. It's OK.

In a way I was thankful for competitions. They would interrupt my regular schedule and cause me to leave town abruptly, giving me a break from school.
We need full makeup for the run-through.
Seriously?
Yeah.
Ready?
Sure.

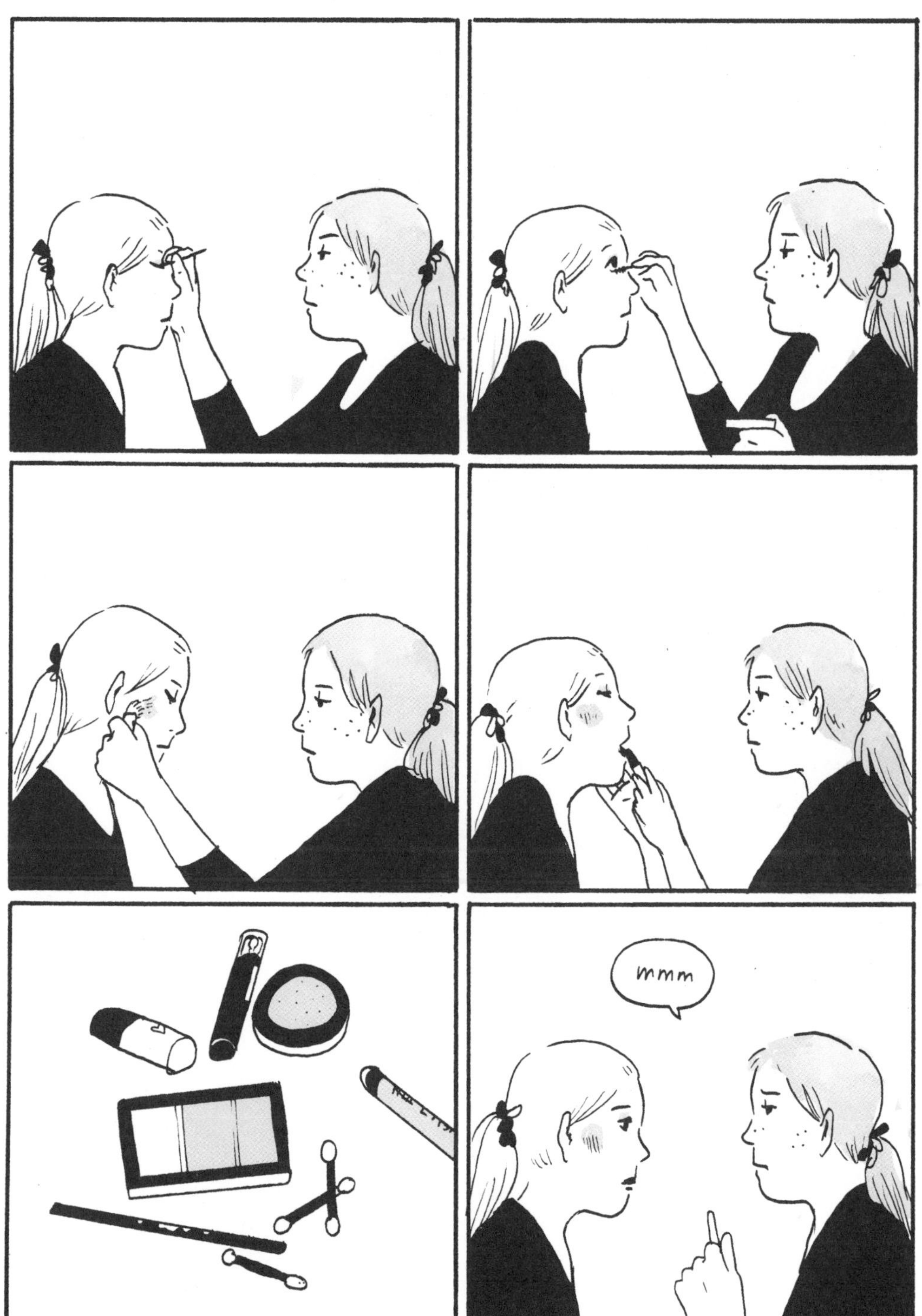
mmm

2
Little more blush.

5

SPIRAL

The only hard part of a spiral was finding your momentum. Once you were moving fast enough and your leg was in the air, it felt like you could go on forever.

While my class was busy with end-of-year tests, I was in Florida at a competition.

Lindsay
can I come hang in ur room?
totes :)
my mom's making sandwiches.

I'd have to take the tests eventually, but to my 13-year-old self, a delay felt like I'd won the lottery.

Let's work out.
No time, we gotta get ready.

Is it the "suntan" tights?
I think so, check the sheet.

Shit. I only have one spare pair.
TILLIE!
haha
Oh, sorry, Judy.

Hey check this out - I found an old pic.

It's me and Caitlin.
omg you're so little!

You're so cute.
Caitlin looks young.
Tillie, you want a sandwich?
Sure.
Mom, me too!
All right, all right
I wonder if I have any pics of me and my old coach.
Look on Facebook.
Nah, don't have one.
what
That's weird.
I didn't have a phone then, so there's no photos.

What was your coach's name?
Barbara.
She was my private coach, different from synchro.
She was everything.
Are you ok?
Yeah.
I gotta do my hair.

Barbara had been my first coach. She was the one who held my hand when I first stepped onto the ice.

But teaching me to ice skate never meant much to me.

I came to her lessons just to be in her arms.

As a little kid, I was desperate for any affection or attention

and she gave it all to me.

Do you ever talk? With Barbara?
cshhhh
nah
She moved away when I was in 4th grade. We lost touch after that.
And anyway, I ended up moving to Texas a year later, so it didn't really matter.

We gotta get to the rink. The team before us is on in like, thirty minutes.
Cool. Let's go.

Sometimes I felt like a stranger coming home after competitions.
You're back late.
It felt like I'd been away for so long.
Were you skating?
Where else would I be?
Did it go well?

Do you need anything?

Could you get me some water?

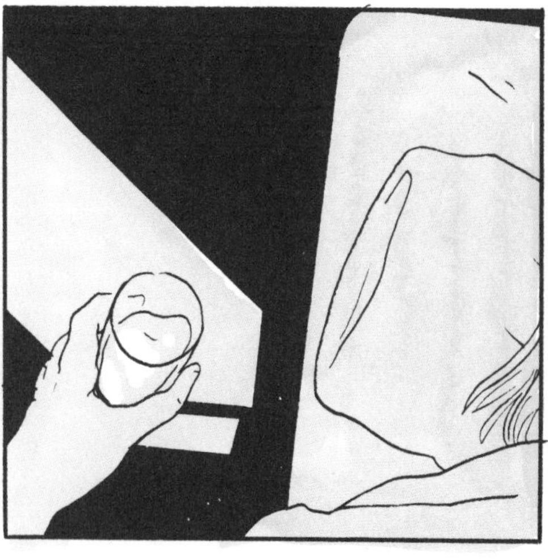

I was so exhausted.

I had thought that I'd hit a wall in skating.
But for some reason...
beep
beep
I kept getting better.
BRAVO!
Your first double!
I wanted to chase that high, that thrill of success.

And there were sparks in my life that shot me out of my tired daze.

The contrast was addictive.
CATCH IT!
No way

The way a small moment could throw me into the sky after I'd spent the day tired and dizzy.
She'll never make it!

I cannot believe you caught that, Walden.

NICE CATCH!

Water break, ladies!

Good game. Shoulda been on my team, though.

I don't think you could handle me.

Every Thursday I broke off from skating to go to cello lessons. My school required every student to play an instrument. These lessons would've made life harder if it weren't for my teacher, Victoria.

You okay, sweetie?
yeah

Initially I had been scared of her, thinking she would be like a coach.

But she was perfect. She made me care about music, and she cared about **me**.
All right. Let's hear your étude
'Kay.

meow
meow

I waited for my mom to pick me up alongside the fence by Victoria's house, which ran along a highway exit.

I didn't see it coming.

I just felt my body fly

and then I felt my face on the ground.

Two cars had collided inches from me. The impact sent me off to the side like a leaf in the wind. Once I realized what had happened I immediately hid, worried I was in trouble. No one noticed me or questioned the out-of-place cello. Luckily I wasn't hurt except for some scrapes.

Something changed in me that night.

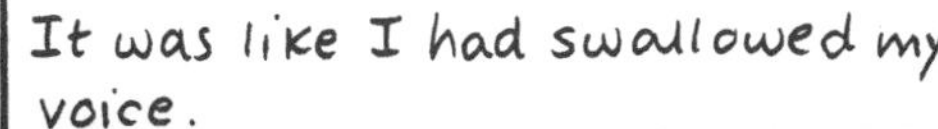
It was like I had swallowed my voice.

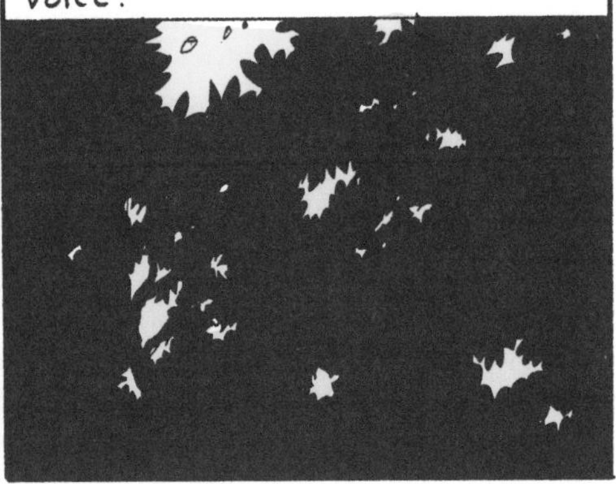

I wanted to scream and cry but nothing came out.

Even after my heartbeat had slowed down, I knew that the words were gone.

This silence spread over everything.

Before that night I had been planning on telling my parents that I wanted to stop skating.

Even with the parts of it that were going well, I still knew I didn't want to do it anymore.
Sorry I'm late, T.
it's okay
How was cello?

But these plans got swallowed up with everything else.
Tillie?

Every time I thought about telling someone, anyone, how I was feeling, I felt like I was choking.
it was fine

I tried to distract myself. But all I could feel were the scrapes on my palms.
I was so scared. I didn't want to get close to anything like that ever again.
click
Cloudy
mrow
mrow
The next morning I found out that something else had changed.

beep
I couldn't jump anymore.

Every time I would go into one I would stop.
beep

I just couldn't do it.
beep

I didn't want to fall.
beep

Caitlin didn't understand what was wrong.

She tried different ways for me to attempt them, but nothing worked.
Bring your leg through!

Why don't we
try some spins
instead?

Check it out!
You got Ally's Sprite?
What did you trade, Rae?

cookies.
nice
Good trade.

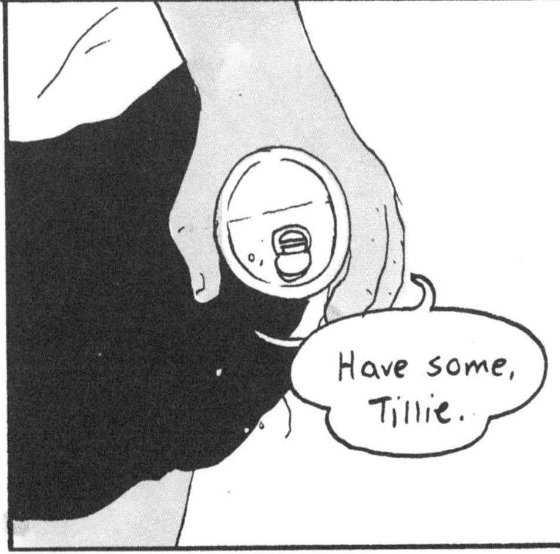
Have some, Tillie.

luckyyy

Tillie!

I had this fantasy

I need the answers to the Spanish homework.

that Rae would rescue me from Grace.

Hey, Grace...

um, HELLO?

It's in my locker.

At 13 I firmly believed I didn't need anybody.
But with my dad, some of that melted away.
Dad!
Hey, T. Great job.
yeah?
Can I wear your jacket?
Can I keep it?
hmm
NK
I'll think about it. You do look good in this color.
You've always liked green.

You don't like green?
Eh. It's ok.
I've decided recently...
that blue is the worst.
But orange is still nice.

I'd been in Texas for almost three years when we heard the news.
They're gonna close it.
no way

It felt like the end of an era. The whole mall was going to be torn down.
I heard they're gonna build a new rink across the parking lot.
Jeez.
No mall?

I felt a surprising sadness. The mall had let us be kids before ice skaters.
Wait-did...

Did you guys read Breaking Dawn?

OH MY GOD
no, SHHH NO SPOILERS
that part
SHH
Lindsay, catch up!

But the part with the baby!

totally

You guys are literally ruining this book for me.

I knew they were gonna marry.

oh man

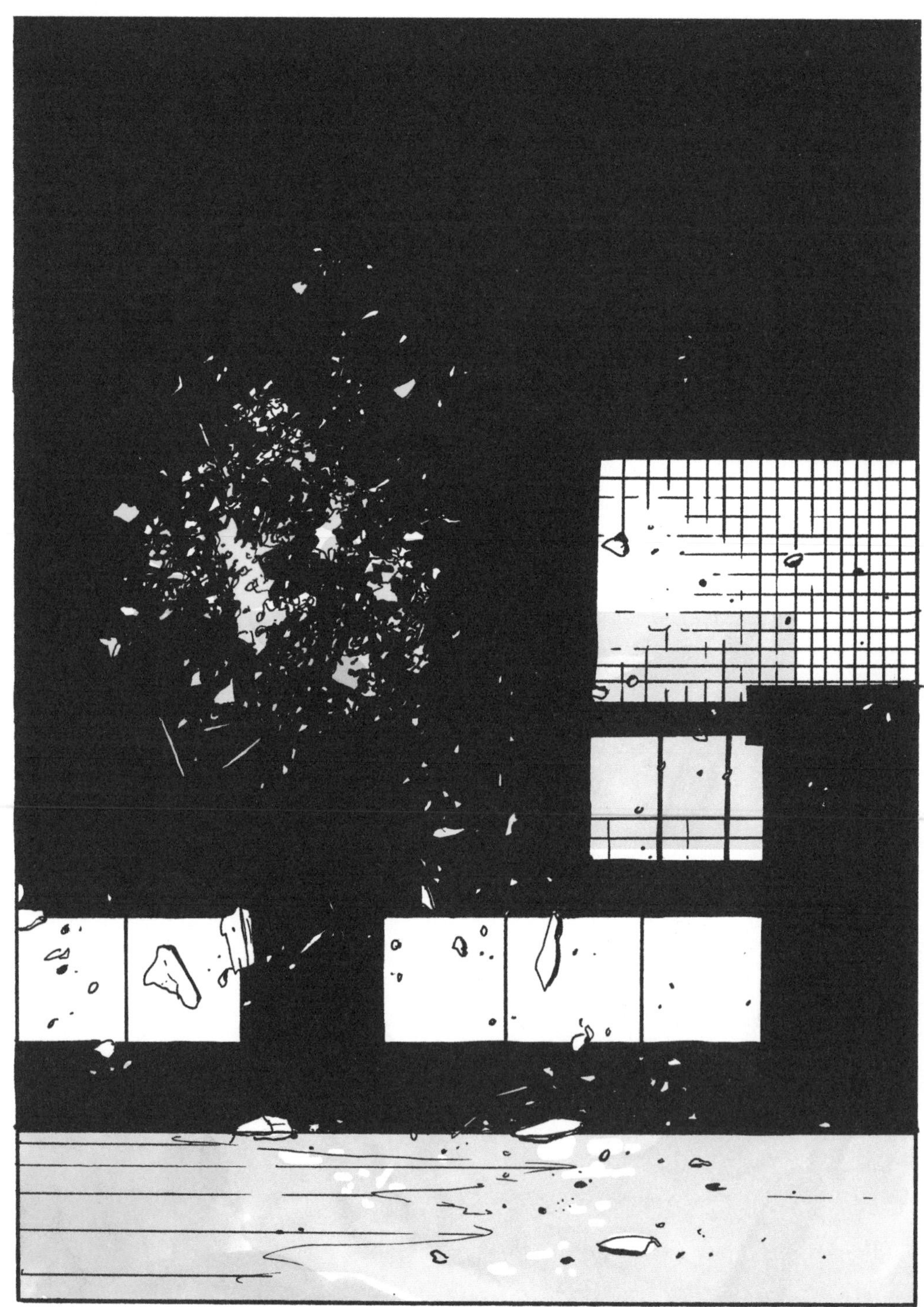

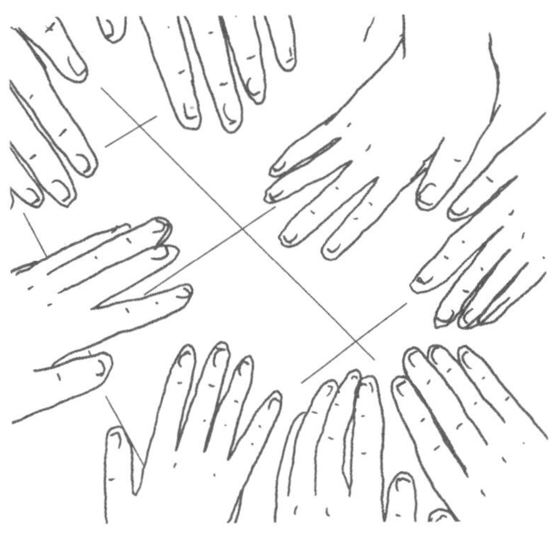

I wouldn't forget any of it.

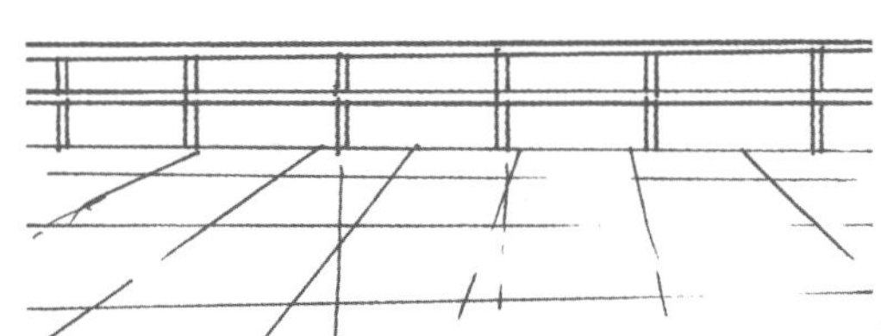

But it was time to leave it behind and push forward.

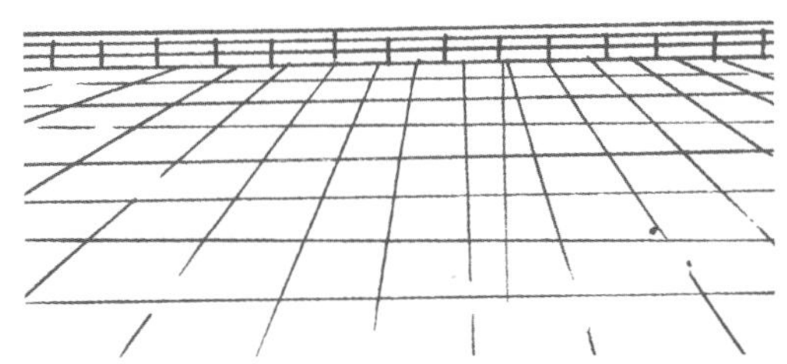

Right after the rink was demolished Grace was kicked out of school. Talk of her had finally reached the principal, and she had listened.
In a way, I wish it hadn't happened like that. I never got a chance to stand up for myself.

6

CAMEL SPIN

A camel spin is basically a spinning spiral. It was a dizzying move and always sent my glasses flying off my face.

Tillie-can we see?

omg!
wow
no way
It looks just like you!

It's not good yet.

Hey
Jesus, Rae, you scared me-

You wanna like... have a sleepover or something?

Everything was speeding up. The new rink was done and ready to be explored, and school was flying by.

It felt like there was an energy growing inside of me, itching to come out.

Is this it?
I think so.

Fucking locked
over here

No one's here yet.

It's pretty nice.
yeah

Is this part of the rink?

Grace was gone.
These rooms are all empty.
And that fact still made me want to scream with excitement.
I had a chance.
Maybe-
We shouldn't be back here.
Come on.
A chance to finally take control.
Tillie- wait!

A chance to be stronger.

But I had to figure out how to do that. I had spent so long just letting things happen, and the idea of changing was exciting yet also completely terrifying.

We should go back.

I don't want to be late.

I know.

Me neither.

Luckily there was a reason to be strong waiting for me just around the corner.

Tillie! Your friend
is here!

Coming!

That night, we stayed in the room above my garage. We locked the door.
Is this weird?
probably

How to kiss a girl
HoW2viDS7

START BY HOLDING HER HAND
HoW2viDS7

MOVE TOWARD HER SLOWLY

SLOWLY PART YOUR LIPS AND...

A first love is important to anyone. But when you're both young and gay and in the closet, it's something else entirely.

It wasn't the thrill or freedom I felt that I rememberit was the fear.

But I had to force those feelings down, leaving my stomach feeling cold and stiff, because I didn't want it to matter.

Opening up was still hard for me.

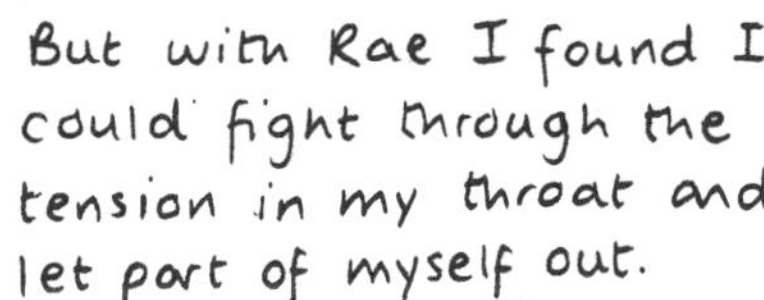
But with Rae I found I could fight through the tension in my throat and let part of myself out.

We were all in the alley behind her house.

Grace made us...
What?

Do stuff.
Like what?

Like take our clothes off and kiss and stuff while she watched. She had a notebook with all the stuff she was gonna make us do.

That's really messed up.
Yeah. I think so.

248
SK8 GR8 TILLIE!
GOOD LUCK!
#skate
#great!
tillie

MOM! My tights ripped!

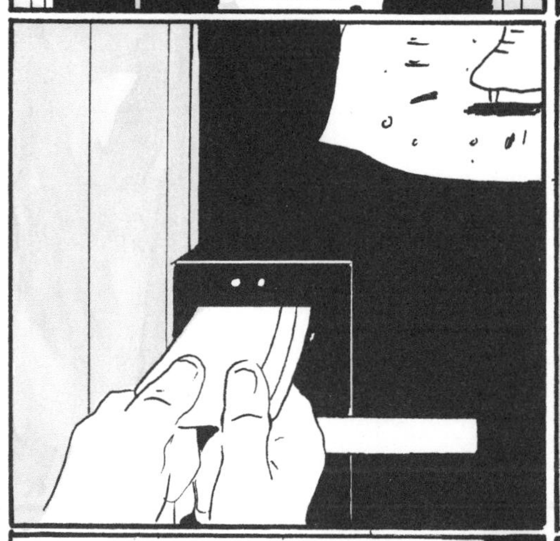

BEEP

Competitions used to make me nothing but tense.

And while the performance anxiety never faded, I started to enjoy my time alone in hotels.

FWP

There were no parents to argue with.
No coaches to impress.
No friends that I had to smile for.

Shhh
Shhhh.
Those hours became some of my happiest memories of skating.
FWP

Even when I got upset, it didn't matter.
I could be upset and no one would be bothered.

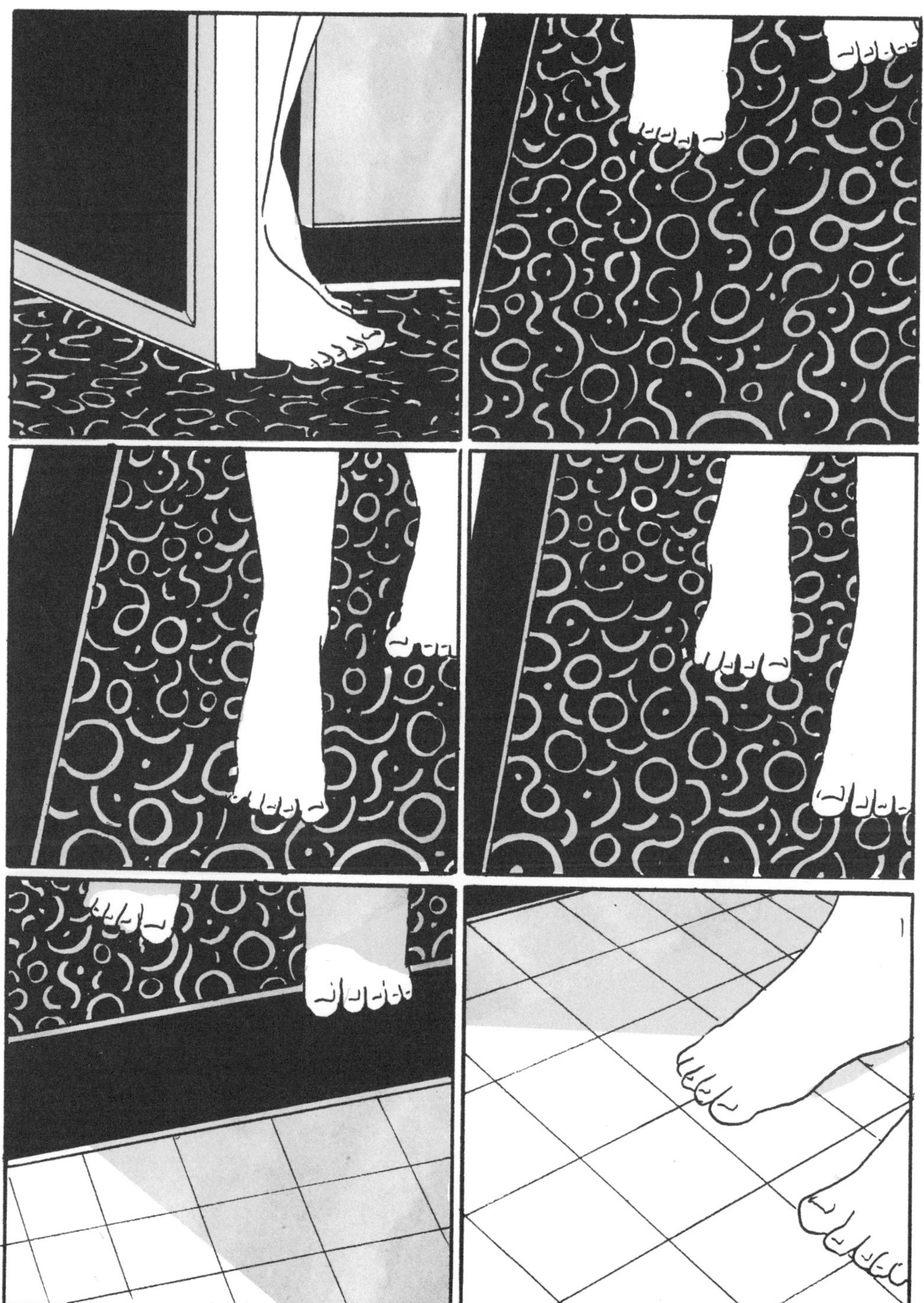

Ribs
Baked
kettle cooked
UTZ
UTZ
HERSHEY

Winning felt great, and I felt this surge to rise above the other girls.

Don't turn around.

aw, Caitlin, PLEASE

Nope, don't do it.

nugh

Ohh!

heh

No!

That's gonna cost her.

Tillie-

Yes! She fell!

OK OK I won't look anymore.

You shouldn't root for that.
I know

CLAP
It just means that if I fall I won't be the only one.
CLAP
CLAP
CLAP

Up next, please welcome **Brian Randy**!

A **BOY**? I'm up against a **boy**?

I'm screwed. The boy in a group of girls always wins.

Relax, not always.

Can I put on my jacket?
No, you're about to go on.

CLAP
CLAP
CLAP
CLAP
CLAP
CLAP
CLAP

Tillie - let's go!

OK - step on.
Now?
He's finished.

Thank you, Brian!
All right, Tillie -
Smile, big arms.
right
Hold your entrance to your double.
uh huh
Have fun, take your time, ammm.
Up next, please welcome...

Every move I made would
determine how well I would do.

A mistake would make my
nerves flare

but a success would give
me a burst of new energy.

My programs were only ever about
three minutes long.

But it always felt like
an eternity.

Great job!
Thanks, Judy.

Lindsay's getting on!

YEAH, LINDSAY! KILL 'EM!
SMILE!
SHAKE IT!
WE LOVE YOU!

YOU OWN THAT DOUBLE!
GET IT, LINDS!
She landed it!

It was easy to see Rae. Our parents thought we were just good friends.
Are you excited?
For what, high school?
And no one was suspicious when I had sleepovers with another girl.
nah
I bet it's like Glee.
Maybe yours is, 'cause it's public.
hmm
I wish we were going to the same school.

I totally own this level.
Watch out for the spike!

DAMMIT
NO, GO UP!

I was floating...
I never get past that part.
It's impossible.

Something had gone right, finally.

Let's all wish our 8th graders best of luck in high school.
CONGRATULATIONS, GRADUATES!
I'll miss you!
Y'all are going to the same school?
No way!
Email me!
I will!
Ms. Ramberg!
congrats
A little graduation present.

Thank you.

By the end of 8th grade I'd decided I'd had enough.

I had Rae by my side now, and I told myself I wouldn't let anyone hurt me again.

But I made the mistake of trusting that the belief in myself would forever protect me.
And nothing is ever that simple.

At 14, I was asked to join the Austintatious Stars.
Everyone, this is Tillie.

Welcome to the adult team.

I was small for 14 and stuck out like a sore thumb.
Lindsay! I'm an adult!
You're still the youngest on the team. Our average age just makes us "adult" at competitions.

But I didn't care. I was finally here among the girls I had always envied.
She's tiny.
hi
Just wait till you see how fast she skates.

Kickline, ladies!

I had to prove that I deserved to be here.

5 6 7 8!

I thought with synchro going well that skating would be more bearable.

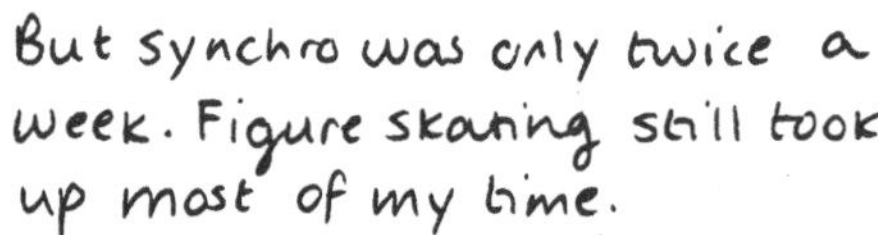

But synchro was only twice a week. Figure skating still took up most of my time.

And that part of my skating life was slowly decaying.

The girls on my synchro team never went to the same morning sessions, so they continued to be a solitary pursuit.

My guess was that the moms had told their daughters to stay away from me.

I was considered a rogue child since I came to practice without parents.

MICHAELA, GET UP.

NO

I was a bad influence, or, at least, they treated me like that.

Their stares and glances were annoying
but I was thankful to be mostly left alone.

I needed to find a way to deal with the early-morning practices. Getting up was getting harder and harder.

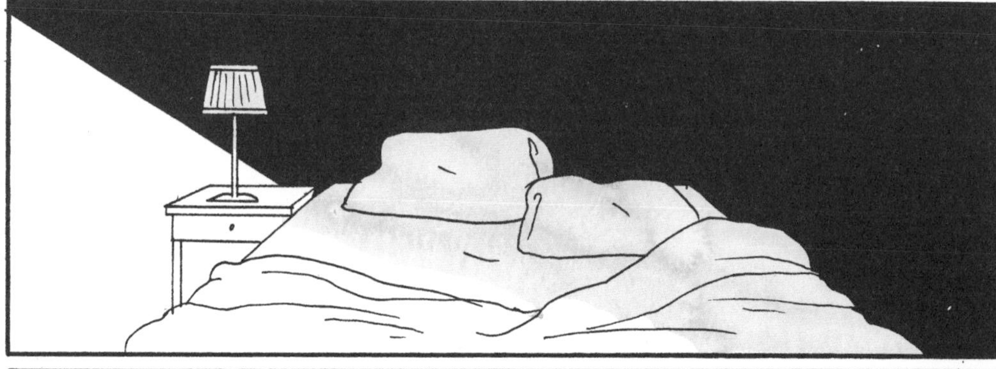

So I made a plan. The best one a 14-year-old could come up with.

I would put on my clothes for practice the night before

and lie on top of my bed.

I would lie there, falling in and out of a fitful sleep, waiting for my alarm to tell me when it was time to get up.

I didn't allow myself to get under the blankets or get warm in any way. I'd let the air conditioning chill me until I was shaking.

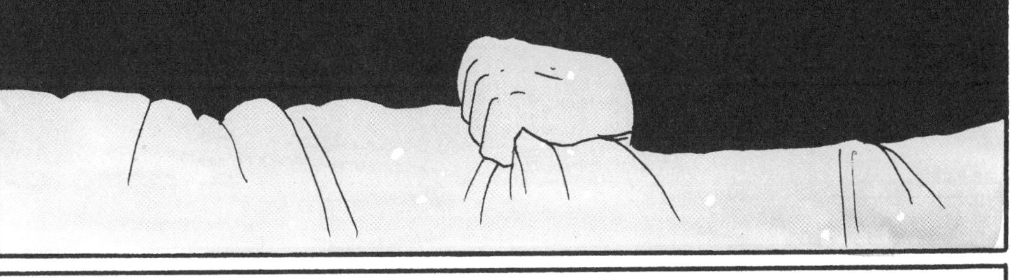

I thought if I was always cold then the transition to a cold rink wouldn't be so hard.

The worst part

was that it actually worked.

7

SPREAD EAGLE

I have never been able to do a spread eagle. My coach in New Jersey had the girls who couldn't do it stand and push their feet against a wall until they stretched out.

But no amount of torture helped me do it. My body just wasn't built that way.

The geography of the ice rink was well defined. Girls claimed specific spots of the rink as their own, and it was an unspoken rule that you didn't trespass in another girl's section.

My spot was a tucked-away corner that I chose specifically because it was out of the view of the mom table.

But one morning I came to find that Mom Island had shifted to a spot closer to me.

I found out later that rink employees forced them to move to a spot where they couldn't reach the ice and grab their kids.

Normally my only interaction with the moms came in the form of glares or comments.

But sometimes nothing could save me from their wrath.
excuse me
Hello. Yes, well - I'm Michaela's mom. I sit over there. With the parents.
um, hi
Well, it's just that the moms and I aren't sure you understand paying for your ice time.
Get up. I'm going to show you.
What?
GET UP.

Normally mothers take care of this. Ice skating isn't FREE. Do you have money?

um... yes?
There shouldn't be a problem, then.

You sign your name and pay here. Clear?
yes

You can go.

Sort everything out?

You ready to get on?

Ok, so you're testing at 8am, so you need to be warming up at 7.
right

You know the drill.
right

Be sure to remember the correct-
right
Are you ok?

I feel sick.

shit

godammit
it's early

That night at Victoria's house had shown me just how fragile everything around me is.
I-
How did she-

She read our **emails**? That's an invasion of-
OK.
OKAY.

Then why did it still sting with with surprise when everything fell apart?
Does that mean I can't see you?

I-
OK.
I promise.

I won't call or email. I don't want you to get in trouble.

OK. Bye.

I hadn't seen her since high school had started.

We had both been too busy. But now I blamed myself for not finding a way to see her one last time.

I thought there was no way her mom could keep us apart.

But it would be many years before I would see Rae again.

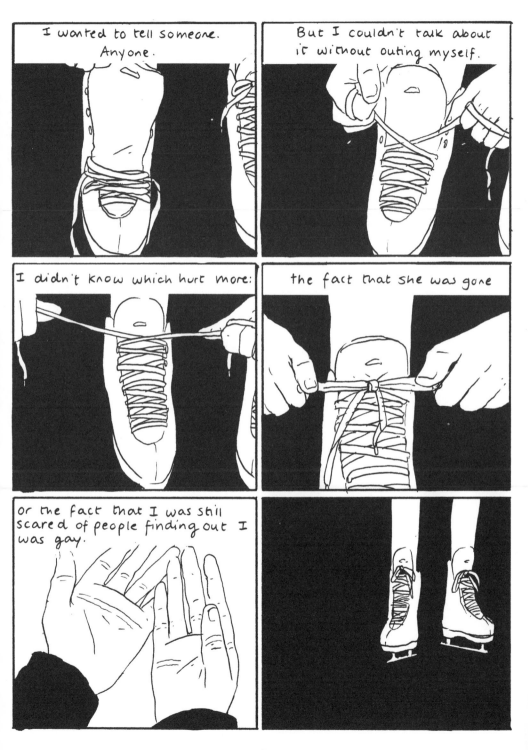

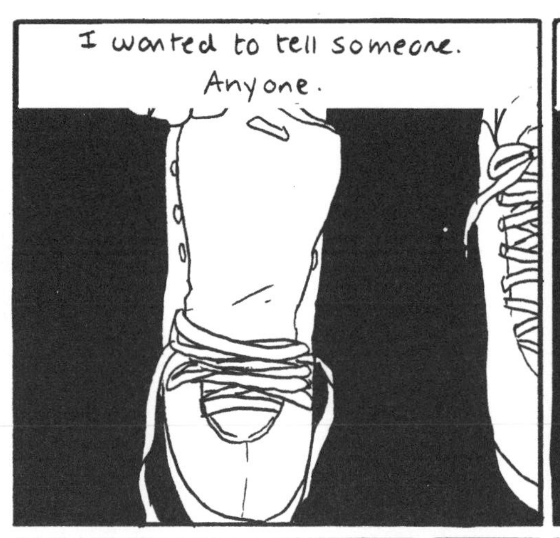

I wanted to tell someone.
Anyone.

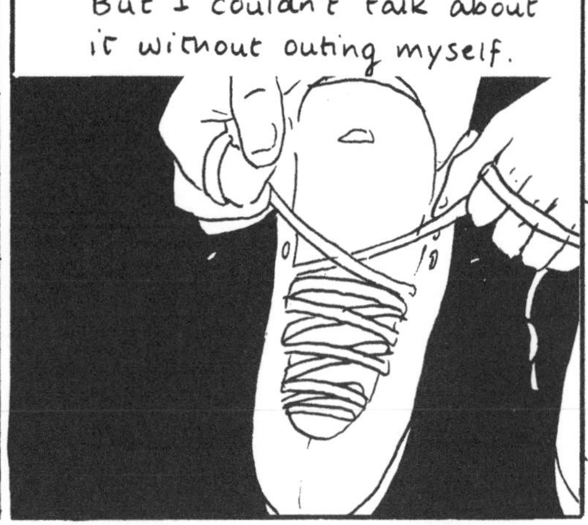

But I couldn't talk about it without outing myself.

I didn't know which hurt more:

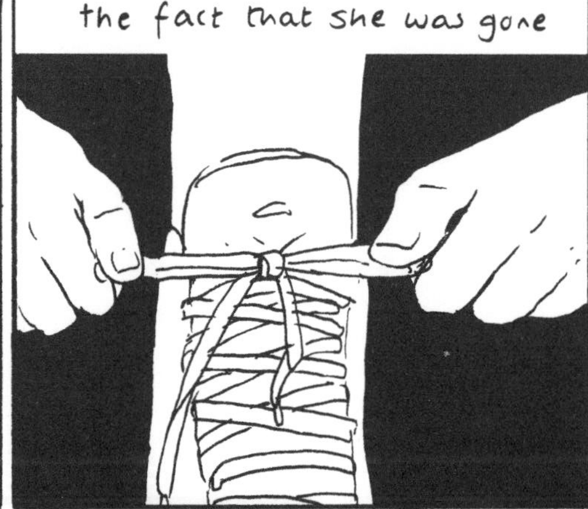

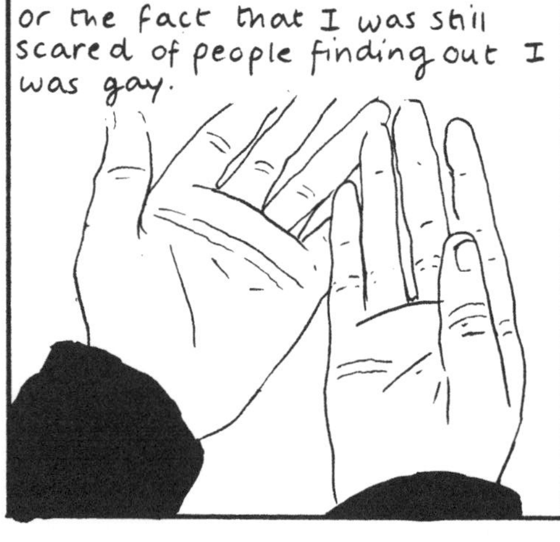

or the fact that I was still scared of people finding out I was gay.

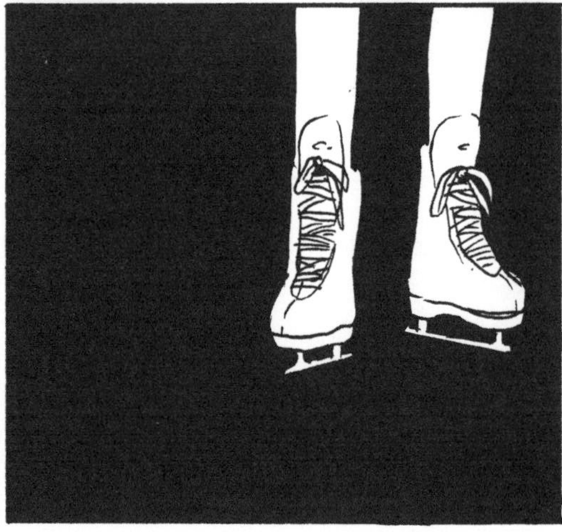

It's going to be a beautiful Service. Y'all should come.
Church?

I've never been.

NEVER?

Ladies - we're on!

Uh... I went to temple once.
Temple?
Uh, like a Synagogue?

Don't worry, I'll take you someday. You'll love it.
There's a youth group, too, a great place to meet young men.
sounds great

tillie
+
rae

I was almost 15.
So, is it true?
I had been quietly planning on coming out when I was 16, thinking I would be ready then.
But now there was no choice.
Yes, Mom.
Well now what, are you and your... **wife** going to wear **suits** at your wedding?
Do you even know if this is a phase?
mom
Don't take that tone.
I just don't know what to do.

I couldn't imagine coming out halfway, so I started breaking the news.
oh
I had a small circle of friends at school. We all had similar classes and had lunch together.
Yeah, um. Just thought you guys should know.
It had been surprisingly easy making friends at such a big school.
I knew these girls would spread the news about the freshman lesbian.
oh, no, no I mean it's cool.
yeah
yeah
I just-like, I'm sorry, I don't... **like** you like **that**.
yeah
me neither
I just wanted to get this over with.
Oh. Right.

Mom told me while I was out of town.
I...
I'm so sorry. If I did anything to... make you hate men...
DAD, NO, of course not.
You didn't do anything wrong.

I guess you should... go to some bars? Meet women?
DAD, I'm not 21 yet, I can't go to BARS.
Ok, true.
Love you, T.
Love you, too.

When I told John, that's when it really started to hurt.
oh
yeah

He was my twin, my everything.
I mean, it's just sorta... wrong, I think.
Wrong?

I just thought you should know.

What'd you do this week, sweetie?
I came out.
like, um
of the closet, like,
I know, I understand, sweetie.
like, 'cause I'm gay.
That's wonderful.

You'll have to tell me about all the cute girls at school.

There are very few.

The last place to go was the rink. Caitlin, Lindsay, the team...

whuzzup

mmm

and I couldn't do it.

Nothing much. Gotta see a tutor soon for the SATs.
why so early

I suck at tests and my mom wants me to be perfect.
ahh

Hey do you wanna come over soon?
Like, to your house?

GIRLS, PRACTICE IS STARTING!
Yeah

There's this movie, Never Say Never. I really wanna watch it.

You could come over and we could watch it.
Oh.

Cool. Yeah, sounds fun.
Yeah?

Just gotta... you know, check if I have time.
Oh. Right.

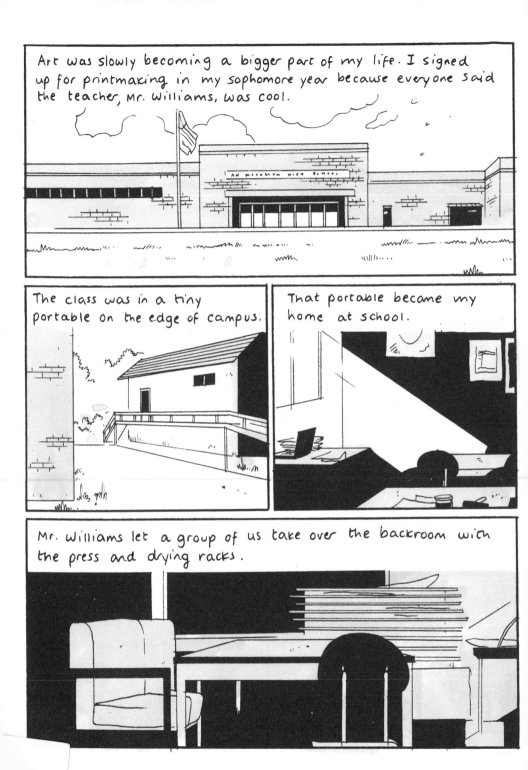

Art was slowly becoming a bigger part of my life. I signed up for printmaking in my sophomore year because everyone said the teacher, Mr. Williams, was cool.

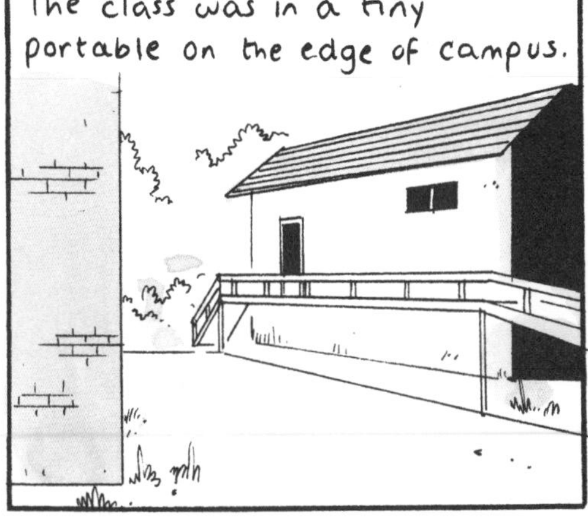

The class was in a tiny portable on the edge of campus.

That portable became my home at school.

Mr. Williams let a group of us take over the backroom with the press and drying racks.

Being gay wasn't an issue with my printmaking friends.
Mr. Williams, it's stuck.
Nice job.

And at home my family was trying to deal with it.
Can I see?
Just you, Seth.

Even skating seemed to matter less with the more time I spent there.
It's just a test print.

It had just become a routine.

I thought if things kept going the way they were, skating would just fade away and be forgotten.
No, you can't see.
Jeez, Mr. Williams! How long have you been there?
You're always sneaking around.
What? I'm a teacher! I just want to see what you're working on
really though
Hey
Sprinkle some water on the ink next time.

Are you thinking about art school?
maybe
I dunno how I'd ever make money. Or if I'm good enough...
You are. And don't think about that.
Do what you love and the money will come.
TILLIE! We're going to Taco Cabana!
oh sweet
Later, Mr. Williams.
See you tomorrow.

All right- is that everything?

I... just need the synchro payment for this month.

I just paid all the other fees, and now this?
Sorry, Mom.

Here.
thanks

uhhh
momm
I HAVE TO
PUSH IT DOWN

Jeez
yeah

That's why you can't wear underwear. Judges will see the sides of it.

You don't wear underwear?
No.

You do?

You're lucky you've never been caught.

Come to the bathroom with me?
sure

I was starting to realize that skating wasn't what it seemed.

I always thought of it as simply a sport.
jeez
What?

We can't wear bras, either.
But with that sport came a lifestyle. And it wasn't optional.

I'll probably need them when my boobs are bigger.

And synchro made the idea of being different impossible. We were told that to be a good team we had to be in sync.

Not just in movement, but in our makeup and hair and tights. Someone wearing the wrong shade of tan tights would cause a crisis. And I hated it. I hated the fake hair, the tiny dresses, the caked-on makeup.

I would complain to Lindsay, all the while doing exactly as I was told.

Wearing nothing but tights, a dress, and maybe some band-aids.

I would put on my fake hair and wear the proper shade of tan tights.

I guess, yeah.

In the cold.

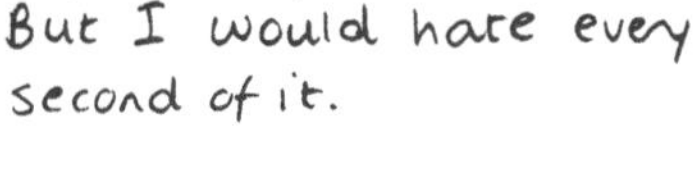

I couldn't focus during early morning lessons with Caitlin.
So, can you add the airplane's number? And production?
It costs extra to do more events.
The same idea kept coming up.
We really need you.
I couldn't fight the dresses or the makeup. And I couldn't fight Caitlin.

I mean-I should maybe ask my mom.
um
but
Yeah I'm sure I can do it.
great

Nothing was working.
I haven't seen Rae in months.
I sent her an email, even though I shouldn't have.
Did she respond?
Nothing was what I thought it was.
It bounced back.
Guess her mom made her delete her email.
Unbelievable.
And now I can't decide if it's just her mom, or if she doesn't want to talk to me, either.

But like... then I remember what it was like when we were together.

Did I sleep too long? You must be bored.
You can keep sleeping. I'm OK.

I never thought anyone would ever like me back. But I really think she did.

8

COUNTER

A counter is a one-foot turn where your entry and exit are on opposite curves. A perfect counter makes a very specific mark on the ice. After doing a few I would always retrace my steps, searching for the perfect cut in the ice.

When I was 16, I tested Novice. I had to get up at 3:15 am to get there on time. I may have been able to fake my way through competitions and practices, but testing was different.
You ready?
I think so.
The judges were waiting for a mistake. Searching for one.

It's just like any other test.

ok. Take
your time.
I will.

Novice was a level that was infamous for judges cracking down on minute errors.

Are you Tillie?

yes

Are you ready to test, Tillie?
yes

Well then. Good luck.
thank you

There was no music to tell me when to start.

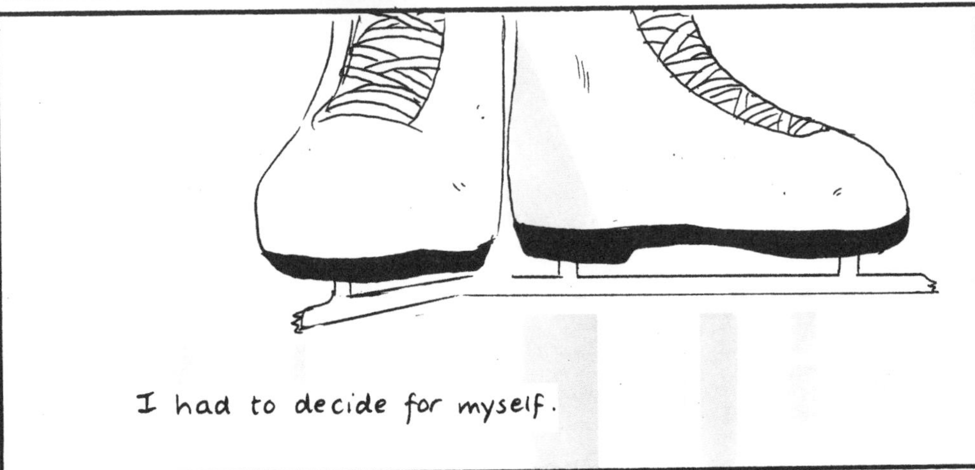
I had to decide for myself.

I still remember the feeling of digging my blade into the ice, straining every muscle.
And pushing off, searching for power.

But sometimes, no matter how much strength or speed I thought was inside me...

I couldn't reach it.

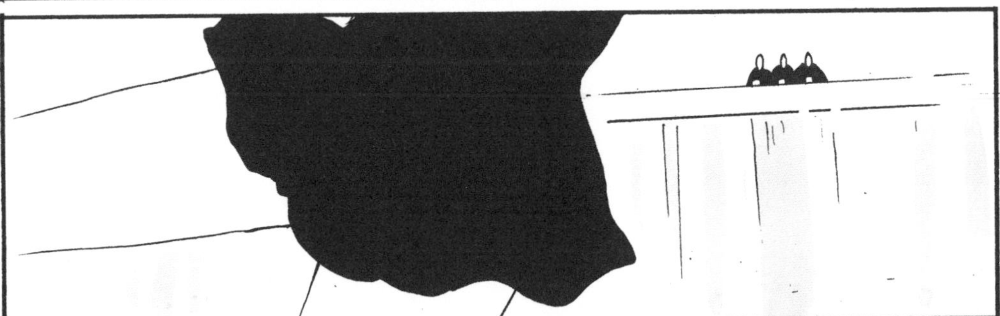

And so I'd have to skate through, knowing the whole time that this weakness wasn't all that I was.

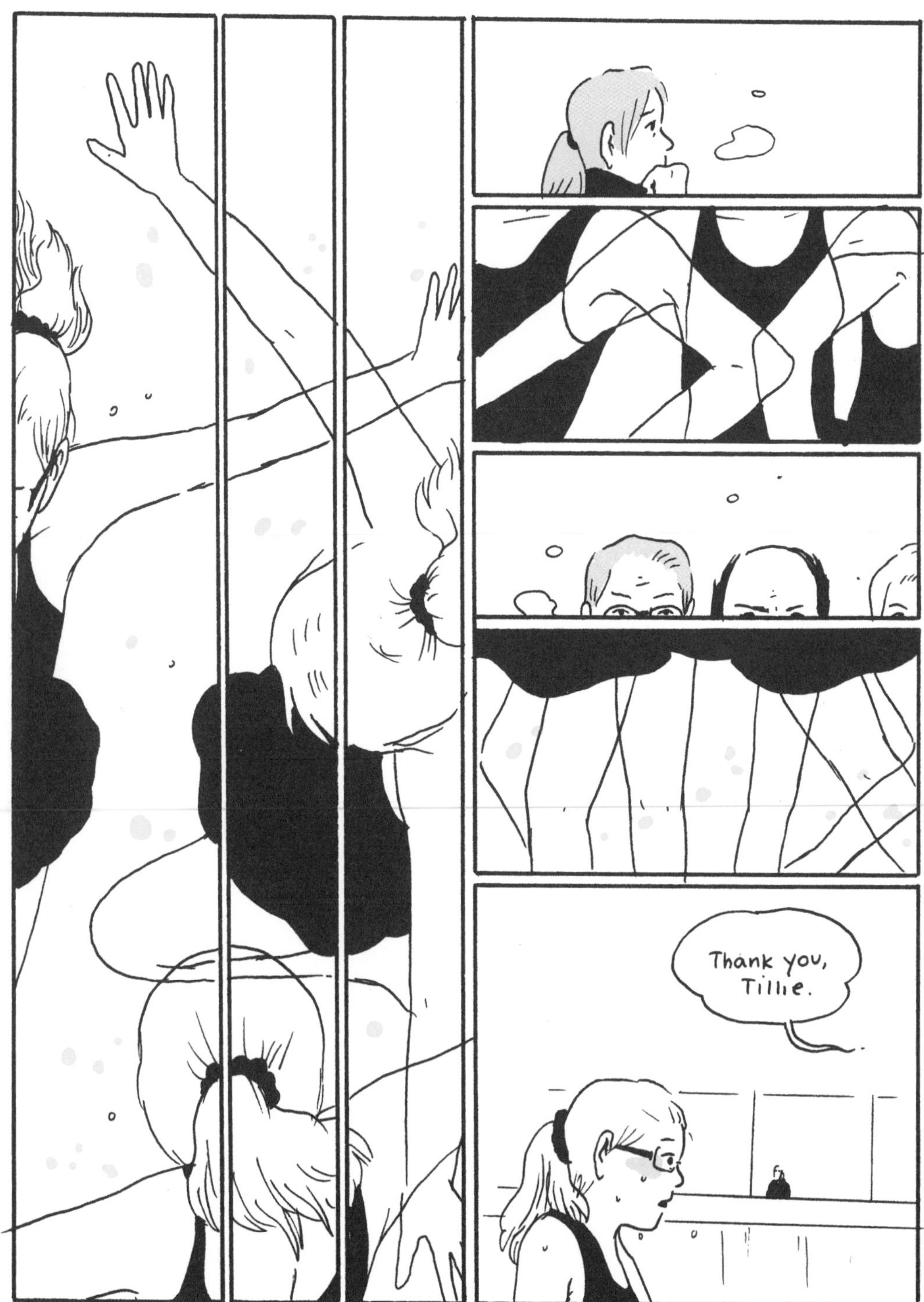
Thank you, Tillie.

thank you

Results should come soon.

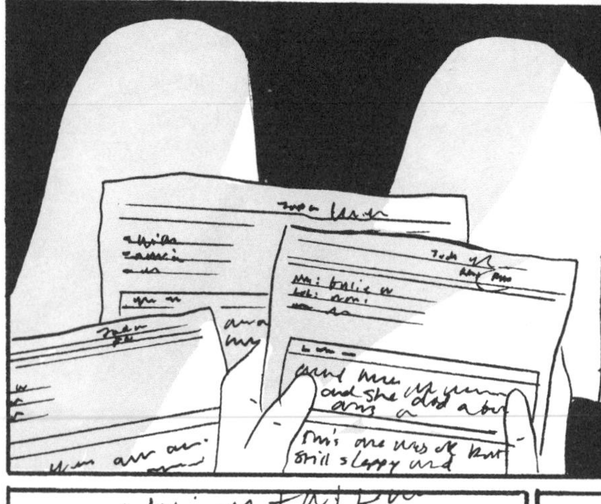

Judge:

Pass Fail

Lindsay was a few years older than me.
What do you wanna do, like, after high school?

So I looked to her when thinking about life after high school.
hmm

Like, definitely try to get in Disney on Ice.

But it quickly became obvious that our aspirations were different.
Seriously?
Yeah.

I knew I didn't want to skate after high school.
Why?
Oh, no that's cool.

What was the point of even doing it now?

The future felt so close.
I had my license and could drive myself everywhere
You?
Dunno really.
and my parents were talking to me about college.
Art school, maybe.
I was even seeing a tutor to get ready for the SATs.
Something **far away** from Texas.
I knew I was on the edge of something new.
You're gonna leave Texas? What about skating on our team?
oh
Well, maybe.
I don't really know.

I was unraveling at practice.
Tillie! Watch out-
I couldn't get through a lesson without an incident.
Way to GO
I was going fucking backwards, YOU should've been looking-
OK-take it easy...
yeah
That wasn't your fault.
That's what I thought.

You haven't written the essay yet?!
God, CHILL.

How're you gonna get it done?
whatever

Ms. Eckor is out sick, and she gave me a worksheet for y'all.
Substitute
Ms Botts

A calculus word puzzle?
So DUMB

Excuse me, Ms. Substitute. I'm not doing this. This is offensive.
why would you give me something like this?
Oh dear

Really? Her name is WRITTEN on the board.
exCUSE me?

MS. BOTTS has no control over the work we get, so shut up and DO IT.

I was always drained by the end of the day, so I was glad that tonight was my last session with my SAT tutor.

It was a useless endeavor since I had no plan to go to college. But my parents didn't know that yet.

Heyy
Hey, Tillie.
How's it been this past week?
SAT
Ugh. It's been long.
well, this is our last session. Let's get going.

"The following sentence tests your ability to recognize grammar and usage errors.

"Each sentence contains a single error, or no error at all.

"No sentence contains more than one error."

jeez
It's hot in here.

Sorry, one sec.
Yeah I dunno, maybe the AC isn't on.

OK." The error, if there is one, is underlined."

wow.

You look...
really good.

shit.

What?

I'm serious, wow, you look great.

It's just an old skating shirt.

But, um.. thanks.

Did you hear me? I said you looked great.

We had maybe 15 sessions together. Nothing had ever...

I never thought-

He had always been so nice to me.

Mind if I sit next to you?
Oh
Sure.
I felt more than just fear. I felt hurt. I thought we had actually been friends.

I needed to get out of here.

Why was he doing this?

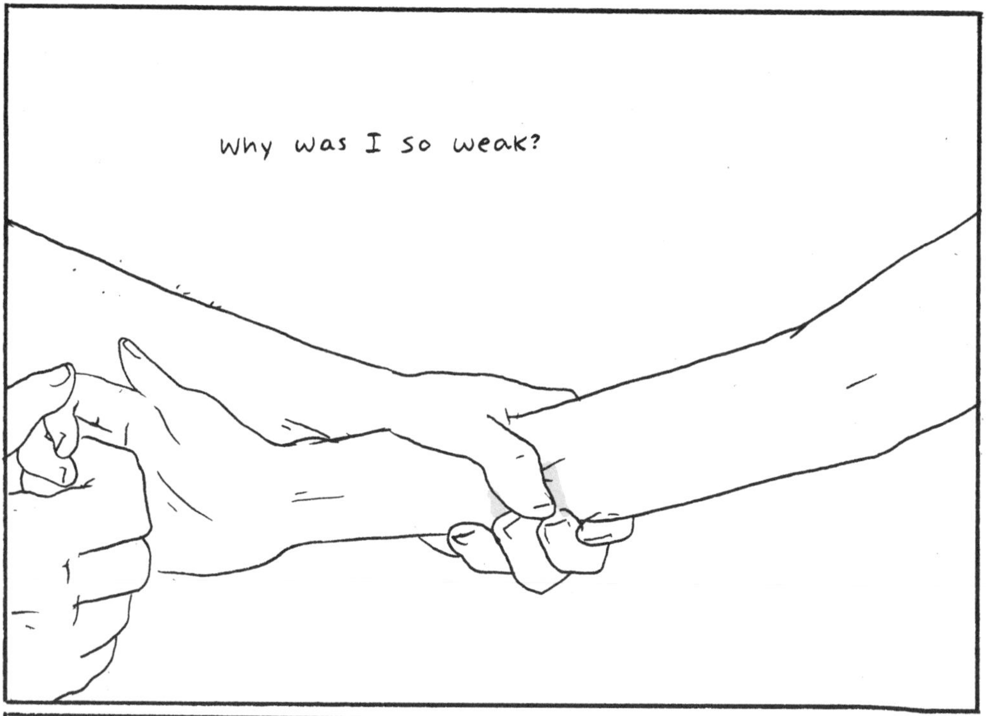

Why was I so weak?

haha

mgthm

stop

Hey.

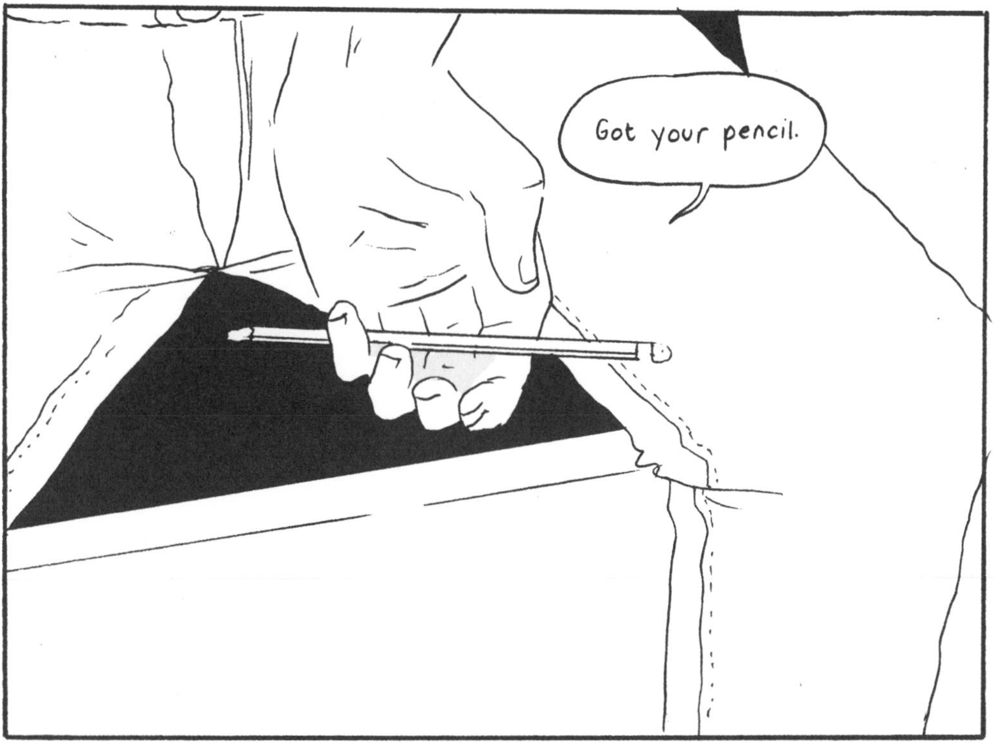

Got your pencil.
You wanna finish that question, don't you?

why did I take
my jacket off

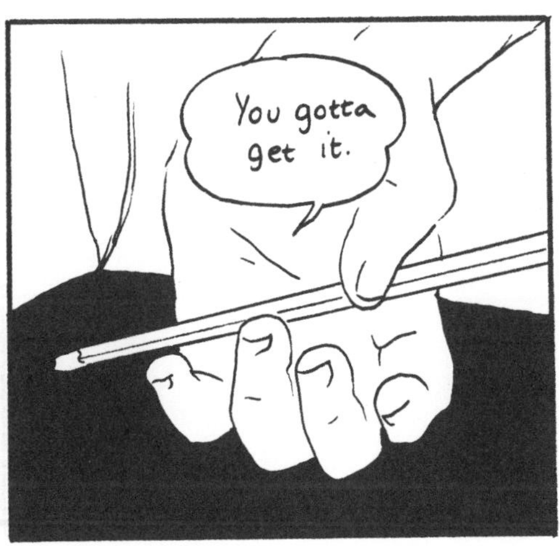

why did I take
my fucking jacket
off fuck

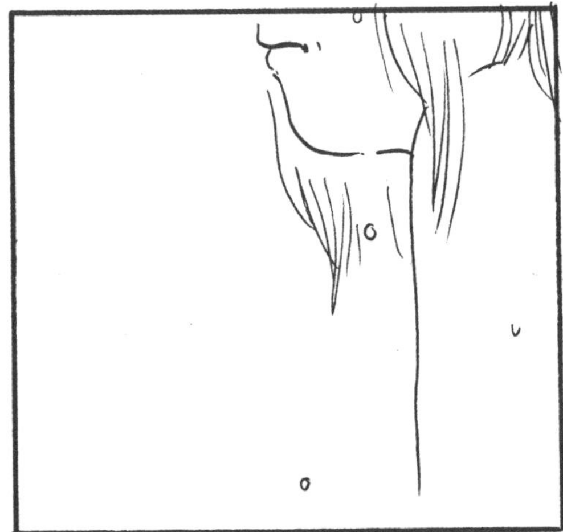

give it

I know now that none of it was my fault. But I told myself for years it had happened because I wore a tank top.

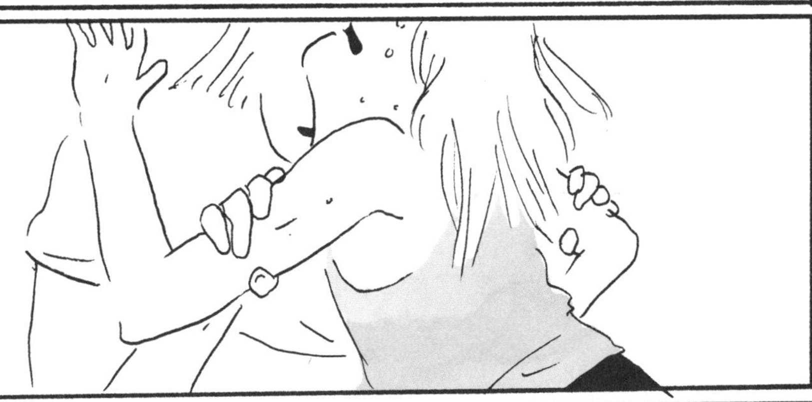

And I did fight back. But I always felt like I didn't do enough.

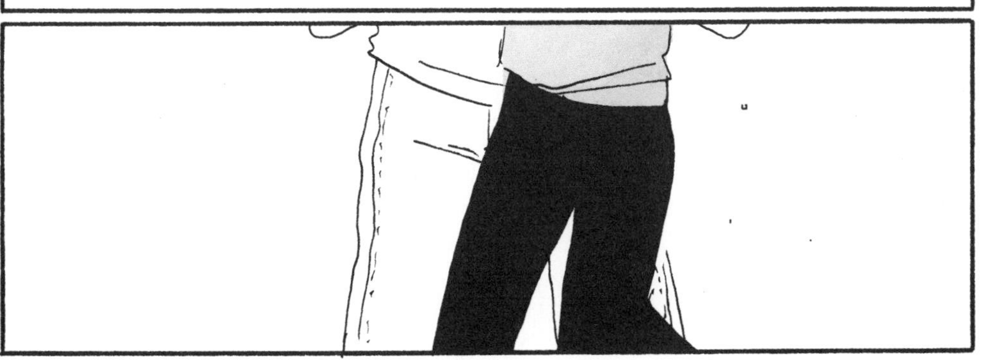

God - quit,
come on.

Christ, whatever. Our time's almost up. Just finish the question you're on.

Hey, wait.
Can I have
your number?

It was nothing. It had to be nothing.

He pushed me around and tried to...

973...
861...

But I was lucky, wasn't I? I fought him until he got tired and quit trying.

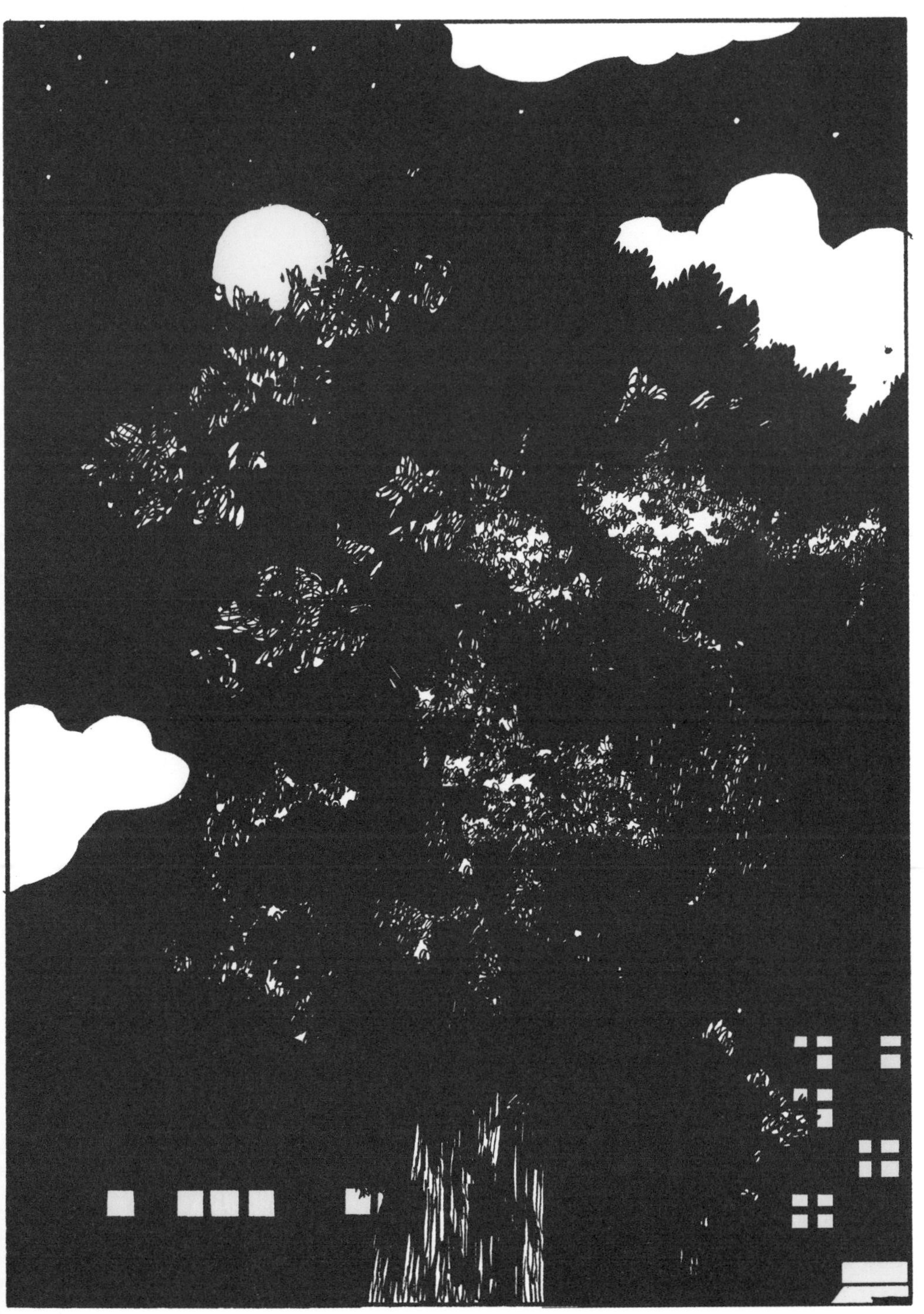

I didn't want to be anywhere. I didn't want to be awake.

So I slept.

I drifted through
You doing okay?
yeah

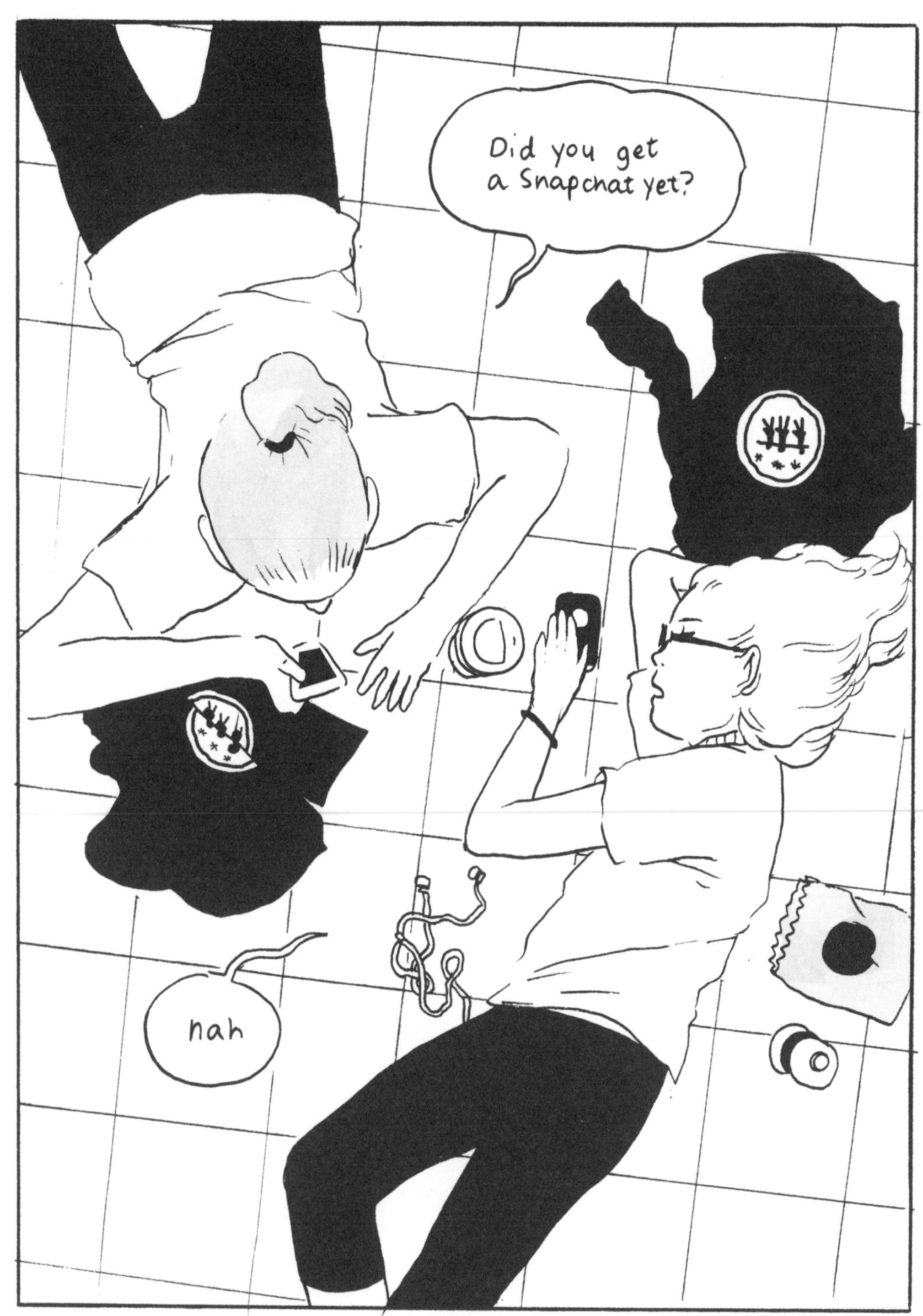
Did you get
a Snapchat yet?
nah

letting the time pass.

FUCK YOU

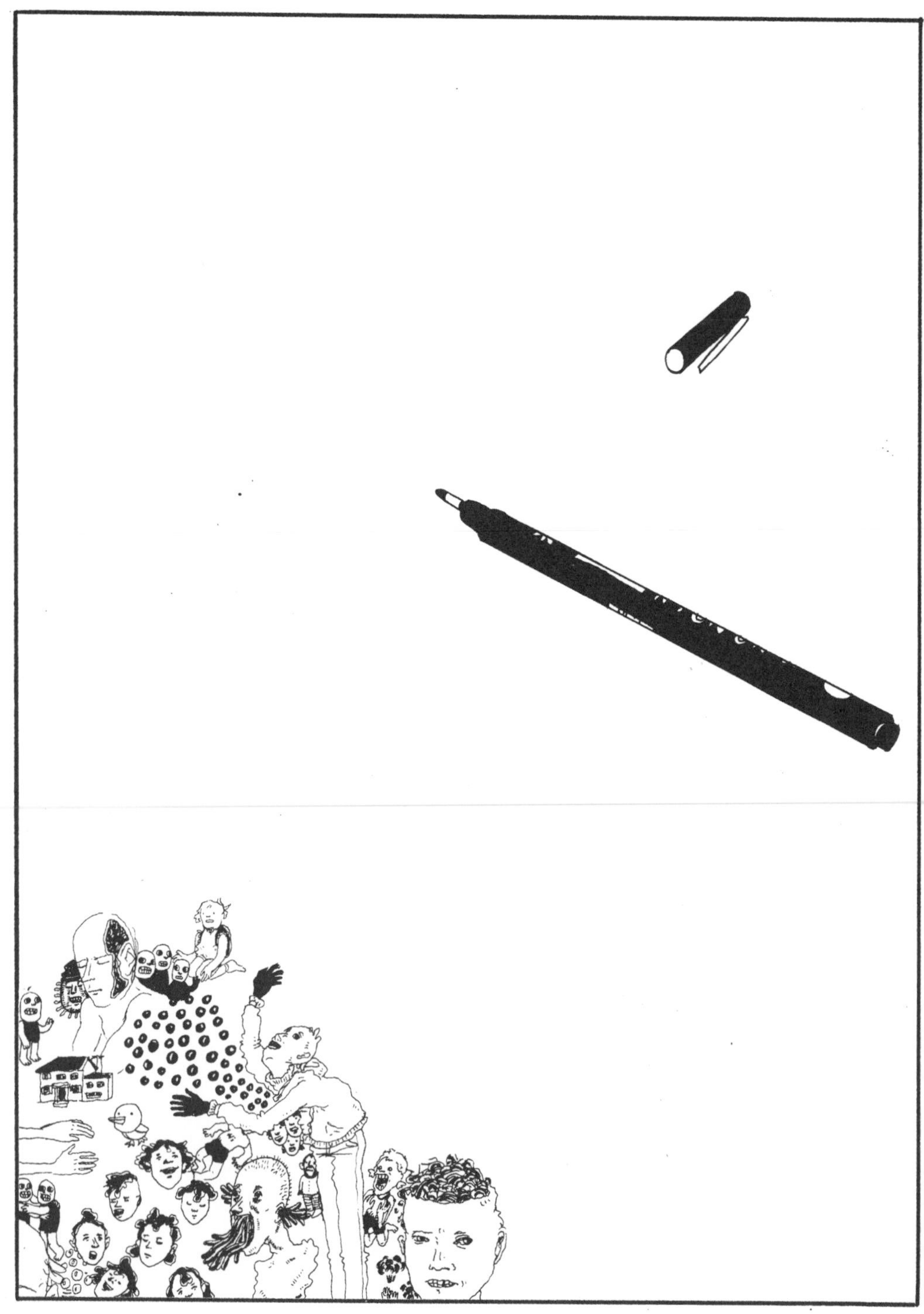

3:02 AM
MY SAT
CRITICAL READING: 740
MATHEMATICS: 690
WRITING: 720

Higher?

Eventually, I reached a point where too much was at stake. I needed to think about colleges and my parents wanted to know what I was going to do.

I needed to wake up.
So I clenched my jaw and shoved myself out of my slumber.

9

LUTZ

A Lutz was an awkward jump. You went into it with your body angled one direction, but to get into the air you had to shove yourself the other way.

Lutzes always made me tense.

In the skating world, everyone was getting excited and terrified for Worlds, the biggest competition of the year. A rink in Colorado was hosting the competition this year.

I never really figured out why Worlds was so important. It didn't qualify us for anything. And none of us were going to be Olympians. We were all trapped in the whirlpool of mid-level competitive figure skating.
603

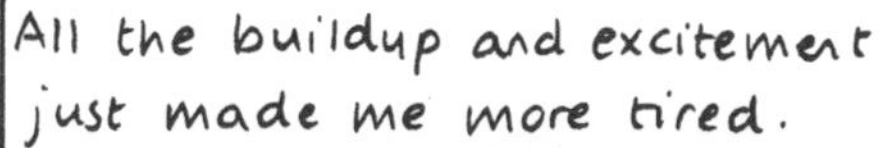
All the buildup and excitement just made me more tired.

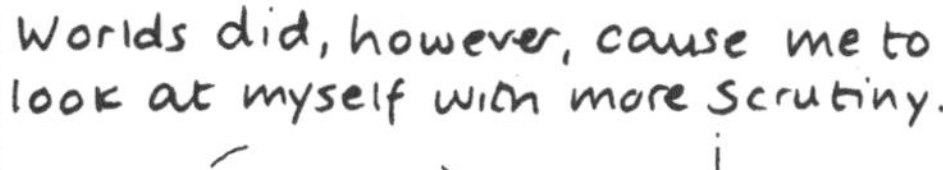
Worlds did, however, cause me to look at myself with more scrutiny.

I wanted to know what a stadium of people would see when they looked at me.

No hair?
I'll do it at the rink.

Hey, Judy
Hey hey

No hair?
Gonna do it at the rink.

This is big.
It's Worlds, of course it's big.
My first program is in Rink B - let's check it out.
CHINA
CHINA
CHINA
RINK B

yikes.

This elevation is killing me. Why'd Worlds have to be in Colorado?
I competed in Colorado when I was a kid.

Yeah?
It was synchro nationals. We bombed.
Seriously?
Yeah. 12th place.
Barbara had moved to Colorado right before nationals.
Your old coach?
Yeah.
I was **so dumb**. I thought Colorado was just one thing. Like, if I was there, she would be, too.
I remember waiting for her to come get me.

I didn't want to admit that she was really gone.

So much of my early years in skating weren't about skating at all. They were only about Barbara.

Sometimes I even think that I kept skating for so many years because I was searching for her replacement, thinking that the rink was where I would find someone to care about me.

We gotta go to the locker room.
I'm coming, Molly.

So fucking dumb.
Should we go?
Yeah. Let's get this over with.

Start the fucking music

everyone, please welco

Who chose this pose. This is dumb.

llie waldennn!

backspin

stay steady

hold check

left outside counter

power pull

crossovers

armsarmsarms

spiral

is my tampon leaking

I feel something. is it leaking can they see the blood fuckfuckfuck I feel something it's def leaking.

The judges can see my crotch.

So can the audience.

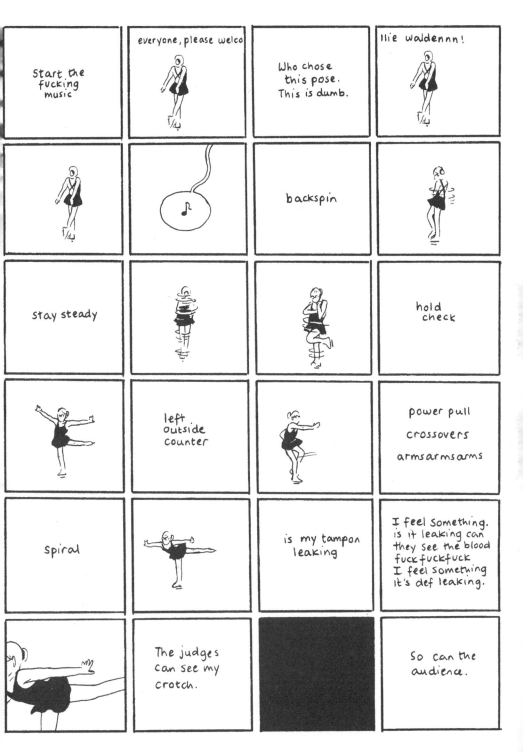

axel
my music
is still going
oh my
god
my coach
is looking
at me
the audience
shit
the judges
I've never
fallen in
competition
before.
you fucking
idiot
you fucking
idiot

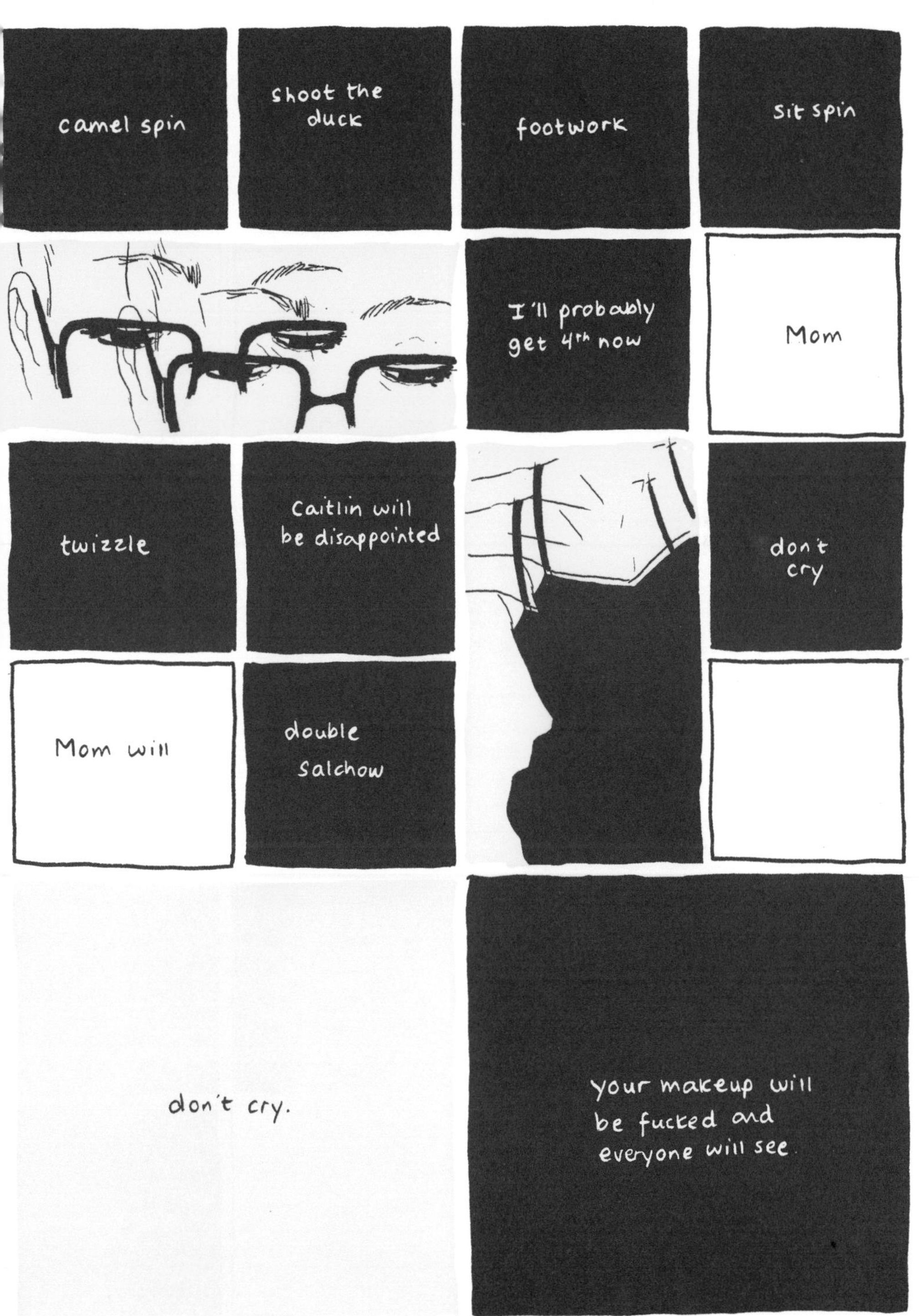
camel spin
shoot the duck
footwork
sit spin
I'll probably get 4th now
Mom
twizzle
Caitlin will be disappointed
don't cry
Mom will
double salchow
don't cry.
your makeup will be fucked and everyone will see.

thankyouuuu
tillieeeee
CLAP
CLAP
CLAP
CLAP
CLAP
CLAP
CLAP
CLAP
CLAP
CLAP
CLAP
CLAP
get me off this fucking ice.

beep
I couldn't sleep.

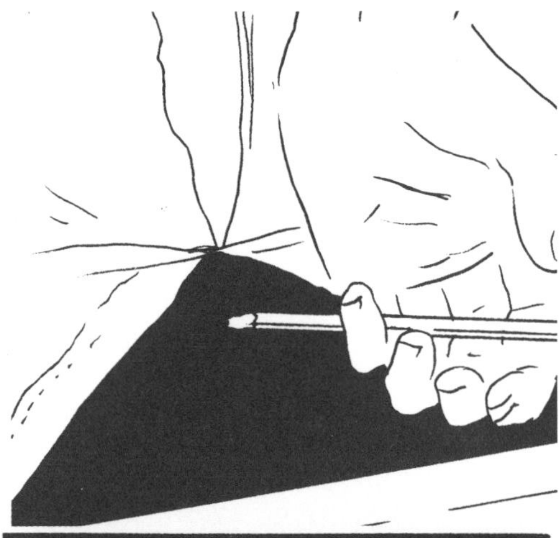

Every time I closed my eyes I saw everything that still hurt.
beep
prrp

beep

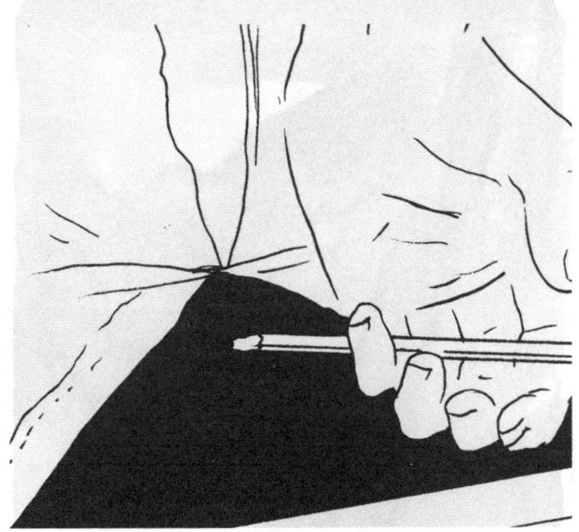

It had only been a few weeks since Worlds and I had barely slept since then.
All I could do to stay awake was grip the wheel.
My mind stretched far back.
I remembered that night when I had been lucky. That night where the car had missed.

The sound of the crash in my ears didn't scare me anymore.
It woke up something inside me. Something that I had been feeling for so long and never let out.

I did not

want to go

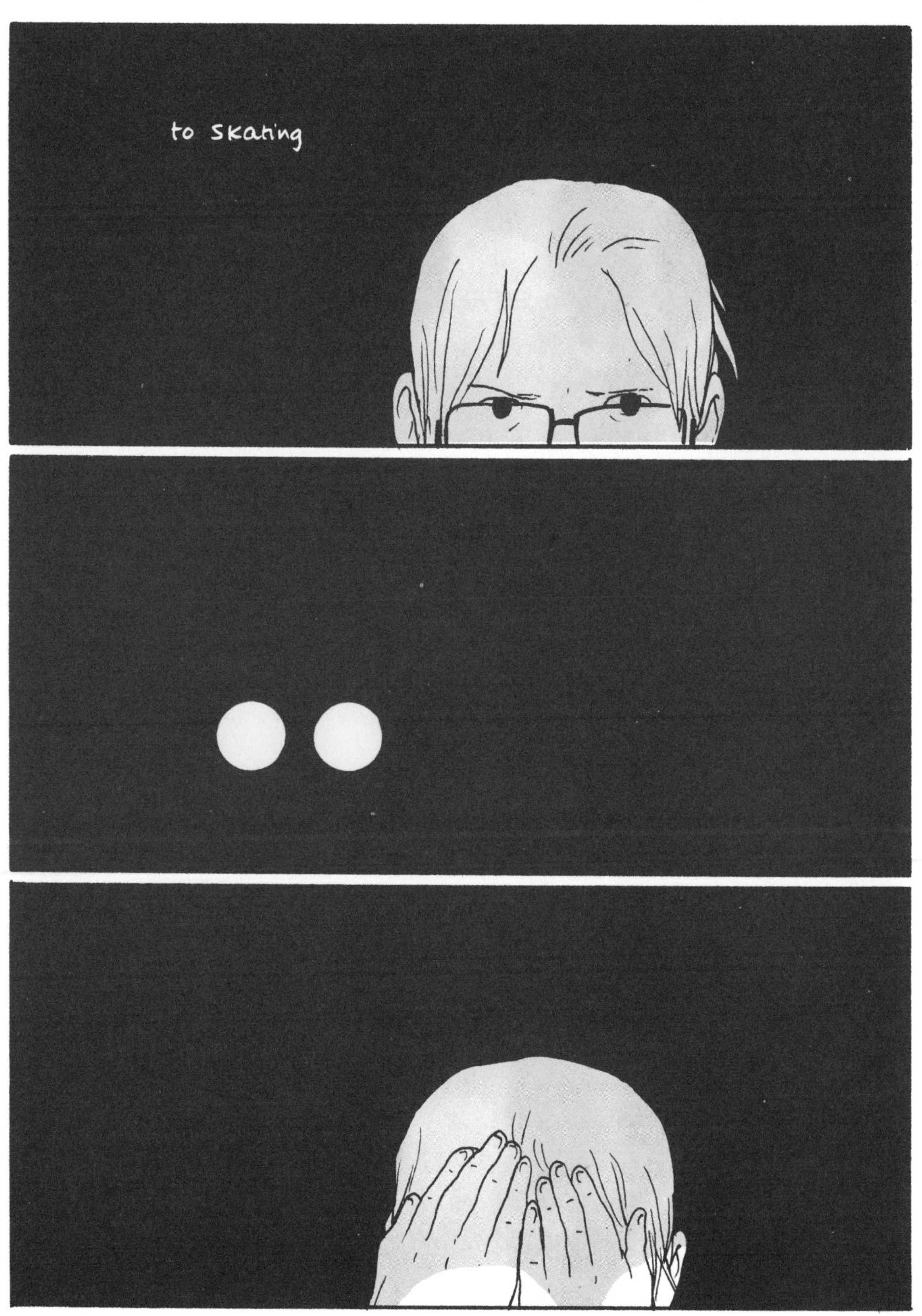
to skating

The car had a few scratches and my head hurt, but it was nothing my parents would notice.

Caitlin
Where r u? Lesson this morning
Forgot to text you, super sick, can't make it
Oh okay. Let me know if u can make practice on Fri
Will do

I never told anyone what had happened that morning. I just fell asleep and tried to convince myself it was a dream.

I had kept going to cello lessons with Victoria through high school.
Play the forte with more bow.

She made me feel relaxed. I could be myself so easily with her. She felt less and less like a teacher and more like a close friend.

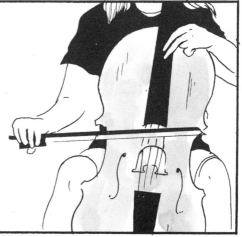

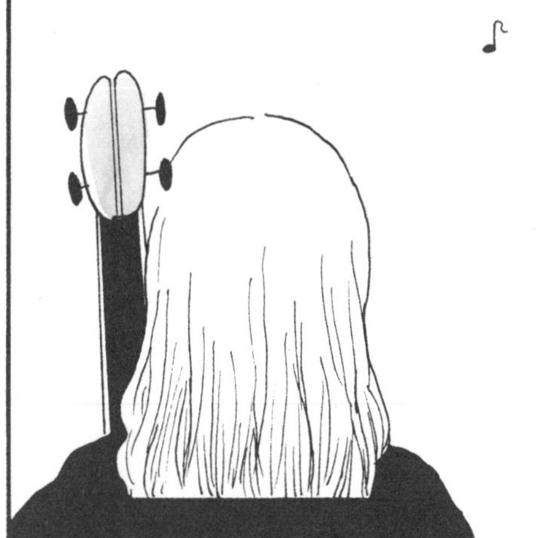
The night I had gone off the road faded into the past as I shoved it out of my mind. Just like before, I stayed quiet.

I felt like I was sick. I refused to process anything, so I just let it all sit inside me and rot.

But when I was with Victoria
That was beautiful, sweetie.

I felt a little bit better.

MOM
Can I play with her now?
No, we're having a lesson now.
Time to go. Find your abuela.
FINE.
She's gotten so big.
It goes by fast.

Oh, did I tell you I got my SAT score?
And?
2150!
Bravo!
John did fifty points better, though.
I thought you usually struggled with tests.
Usually, yeah.
I just did well cause I worked with a tutor.
You know, he... he was...
What?

I mean, it's nothing. It feels fuzzy now...
I only realized later that...
he must've planned it.
Did I do something to make him think...
what?
Sorry, I don't really know what it was...
what happened?
...

Ready?

PASS
FAIL
PASS
FAIL
US FIGURE
SKATING
NOVICE MOVES

congratulations.

10

TWIZZLE

I learned to do a twizzle when I was about 6. It was simple. You push forward on one foot and rotate once.

That was it.

For some reason they always made me laugh. Something about the quick spinning motion made the blood rush to my head, making me usually burst out in giggles.

Mom.

I'm done
with skating.

I quit.

I was 17. It was the summer
before 12th grade.

I had been skating for
twelve years.

You have to tell Caitlin.

Now we can at least save some money.

It made me so angry.

How easy it was.

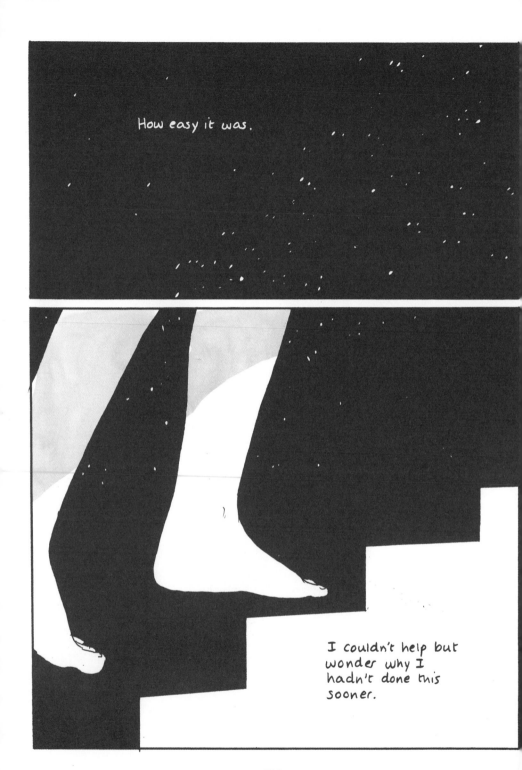

But I didn't have an answer.

To: Caitlin

From: tillie@yahoo.com

Subject: Skating

Caitlin,

I've decided to stop skating. My next year of high school is too busy, so I won't have time to skate. Please don't be mad.

Tillie

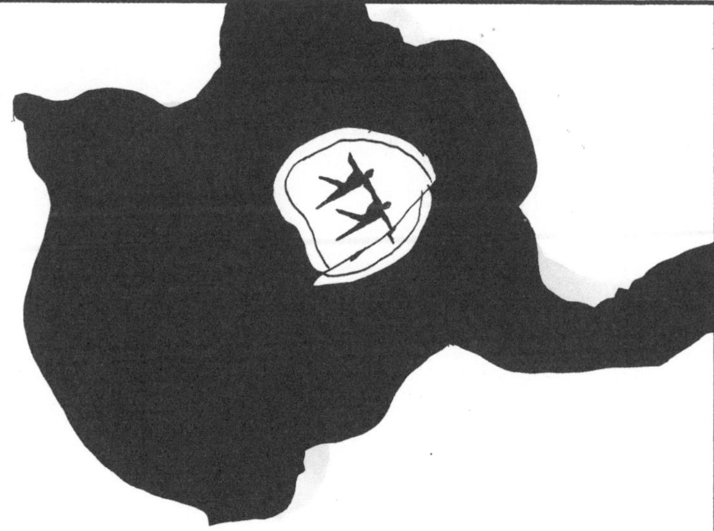

Even now, I'm still not sure.

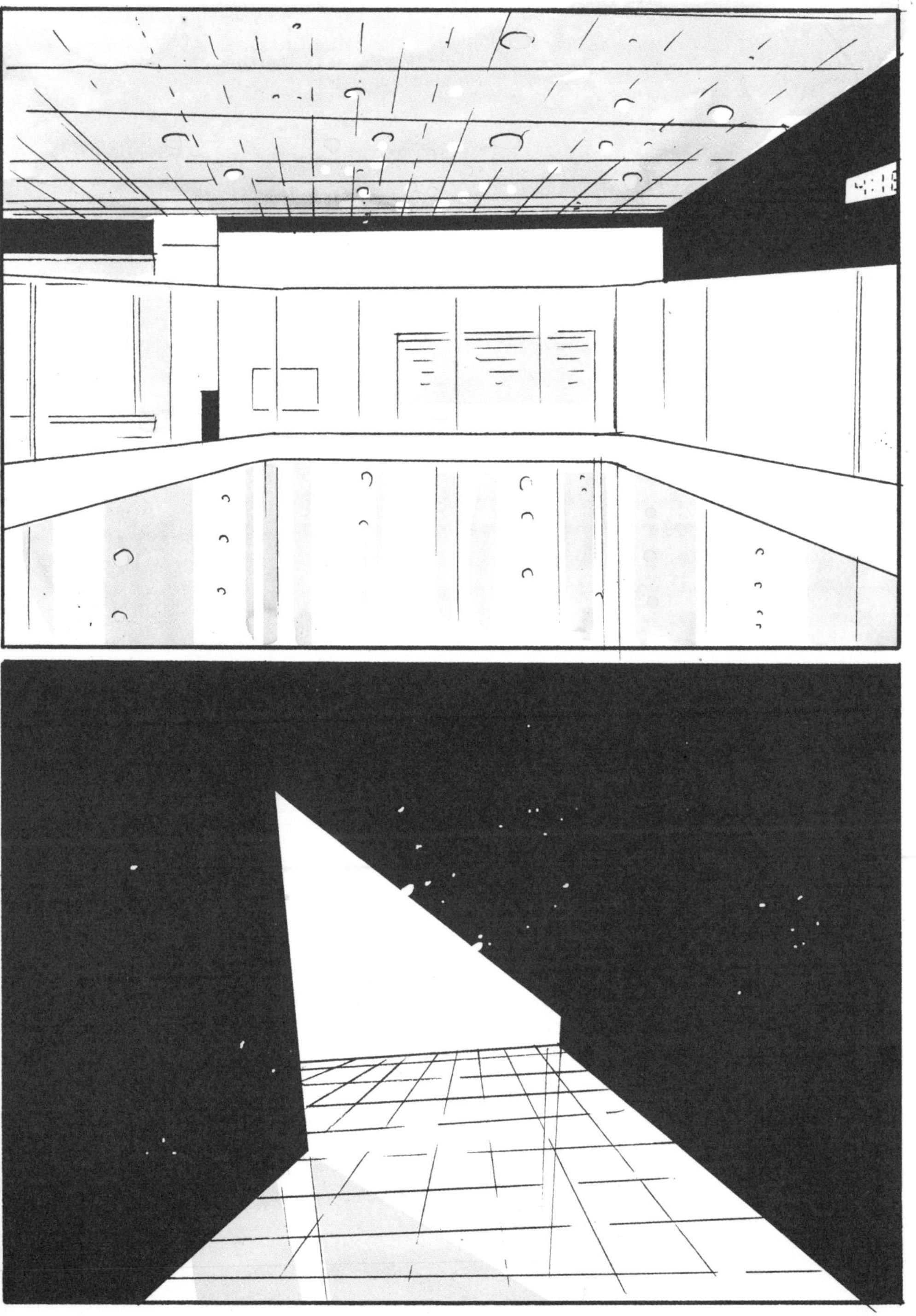

Are you sure about this?
Yes.

Since you're here, do you want one last lesson?
Sure.

I didn't want to skate. But I couldn't say no to Caitlin. Not when she looked so sad.
You can always come back.

I would never see Caitlin, or anyone from this rink, again.

I skated off the ice so fast that I tripped when my blade slid onto the ground.

To top it all off, I made it out that morning without paying for the session. The mom table glared at me the whole way out.

I cried the whole way home,
with my eyes wide open.

It's hard to decide.
There are no schools you like?
Not really.
I don't think I want to go to college. My parents aren't pleased.

Well, you seem very confident in your plans.
Haha, I hope so...
I think I might do something with art.
You've always liked it, haven't you?
I dunno. I don't feel this huge passion. It's just... when I start a drawing, I want to finish it.

geez
This is an unhealthy amount of medals.
♪

Lindsay.

I didn't know what to say to her.
♪

We had been by each other's side for six years.

And that whole time I had never been a good friend to her.

I never really got to know her, and I never let her get close to me.

I clung to her only because I was too afraid to face practices and competitions alone.

And I didn't know how to tell her I was sorry.

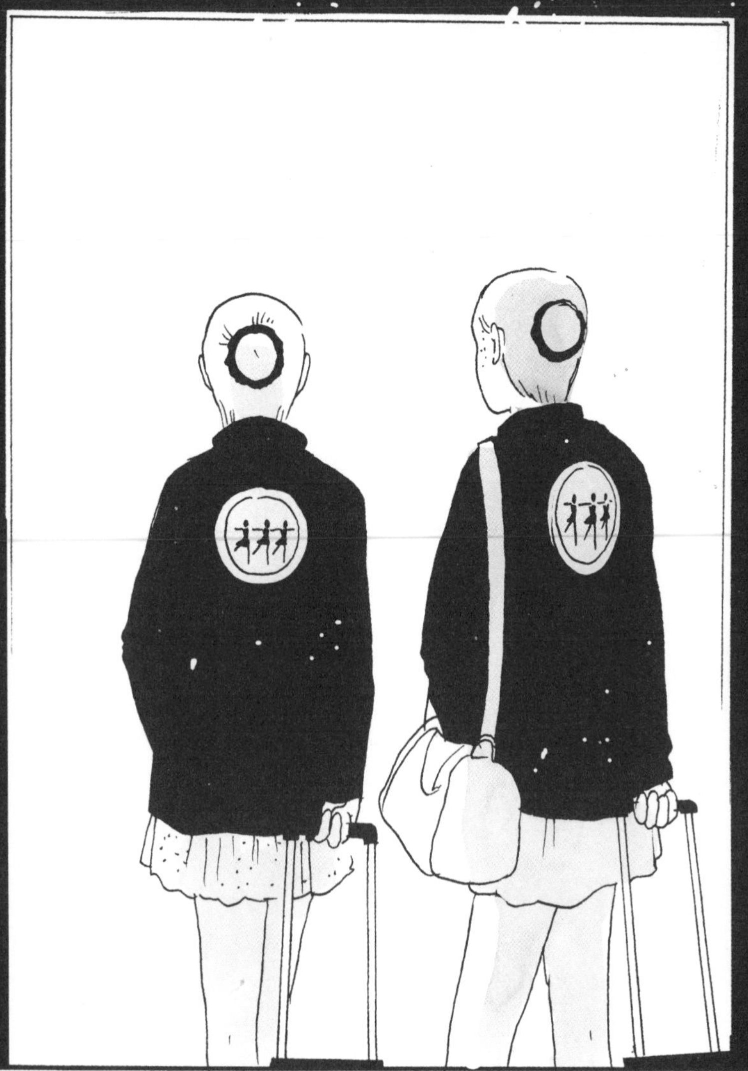

It's been almost two years since I quit. I had sworn to myself that I would never skate again, yet here I am.

But I don't think I really came here to skate.

I just had to prove to myself that I could leave.

Today when I try and wrap my head around all those chaotic years, one memory keeps rising to the surface.

Not a sad memory, not one of exhaustion or nerves. But one that is sticky and sweet and still sends chills through me.

It was the Cape Cod Classic competition.
Molly, Tillie, nice of you to join us.
sorry
All right, ladies. Before we leave the hotel we need full makeup and dresses on. Remember to pack-

The lights went out,
the building shook,
and 20 ice skaters
screamed at the top
of their lungs.

A hurricane had landed right on top of us.

As soon as the shock wore off, excitement spread through us.
THE HOTEL'S GONNA FALL OVER!
Let's go!
RUN AWAY!

We all took off running through the dark, trembling hotel. It was the first time I remember our coach had no control over us.

It felt so good to scream.

Are we gonna be OK?

We'll be fine.

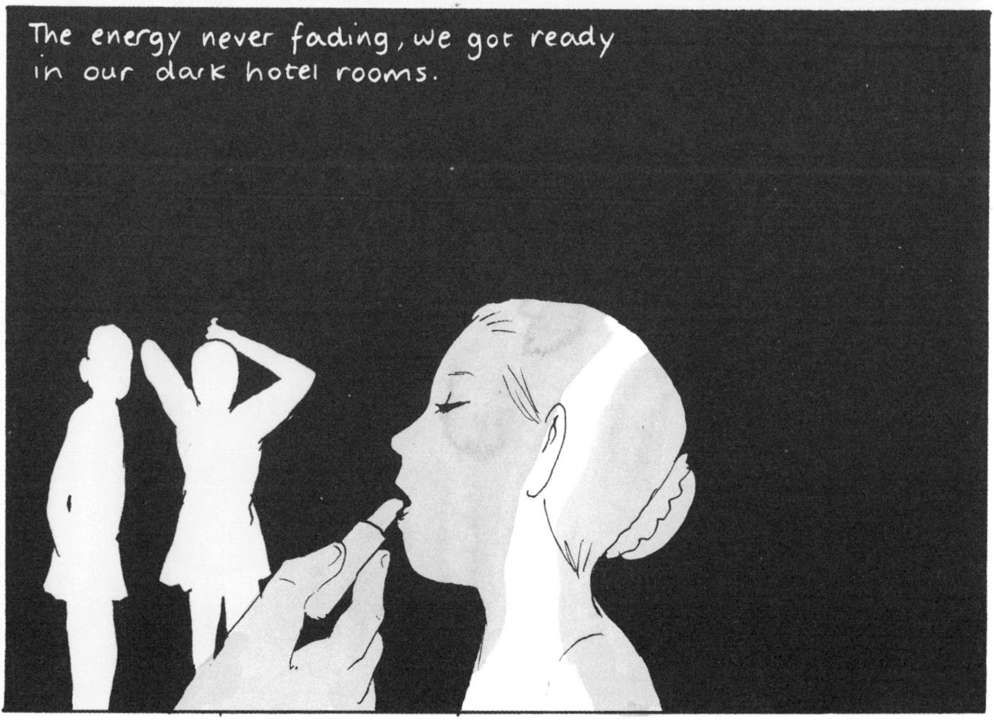

The energy never fading, we got ready in our dark hotel rooms.

Somehow we all made it to the rink in one piece. Still giddy and shivering, we started our program.

and I could still hear the rain pounding relentlessly on the roof of the rink

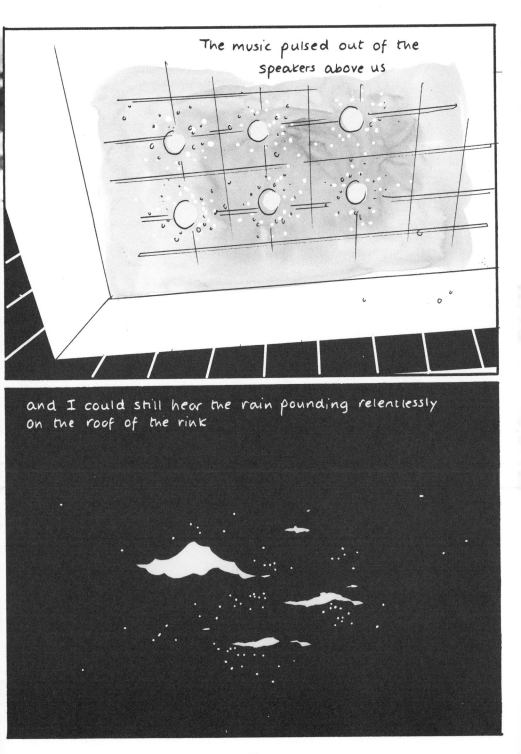

and I couldn't help but smile.

Author's note

I drive by the ice rink I used to skate at all the time. It just so happens that I live pretty close to it, so I can't really avoid it. While I was making this book, it made me tense. I didn't want to look at it. You might think that while making a memoir you'd want to reconnect to the places of your past, but that's not how it worked for me. I avoided photographs; I avoided the people and places in this story the entire time. I think for some people the purpose of a memoir is to really display the facts, to share the story exactly how it happened. And while I worked to make sure this story was as honest as possible, that was never the point for me. This book was never about sharing memories; it was about sharing a feeling. I don't care what year that competition was or what dress I was actually wearing; I care about how it felt to be there, how it felt to win. And that's why I avoided all memorabilia. It seemed like driving to the rink to take a look or finding the pictures from my childhood iPhone would tell a different story, an external story. I wanted every moment in this book to come from my own head, with all its flaws and inconsistencies.

What has surprised me most about this book, especially looking back, is that it ended up not being about ice-skating at all. I charged into this story armed with memories of hair gel and screaming mothers, ready to do my tell-all about the seedy world of glittering young ice skaters. But with each memory that I started to put on the page, a new narrative emerged. I realized that more than just ability goes into being an ice skater. Your life outside the rink shapes how you skate. Landing a jump was never about whether or not I knew how to do it—I did. It was about whether I was ready to, whether I felt like I had enough control to land it. And what was going on in my life shaped the answers to those questions. That's the reason I included a lot of other narratives besides just the skating into the book. The hard part was figuring out which parts of my life influenced my skating. I figured out eventually that most events that involved something physical had an effect. The car wreck, the bullying come to mind. Other events, like coming out, weren't tangible like those other memories. But they involved identity and my understanding of who I was. I think that affected my skating because when you perform you have to put a version of yourself forward for the audience to see. And that becomes a hard task when your idea of yourself is constantly changing and being made anew.

People ask me all the time "What's this book really about?" I still say ice-skating, mostly because it's the simplest answer. But it really feels like such a huge question—what is this book about? I'm the type of creator who is happy making a book without all the answers. I don't need to understand my past fully in order to draw a comic about it. And now that this is a book that other people will read, I feel like it's not really my turn to answer that question. It's for the reader to decide, to speculate, to guess. It reminds me of how in English class in high school we would always talk about the author's intentions in every moment. And I used to always wonder if there was ever an author who really didn't mean any of it, and the meaning found its way in by accident. I think I'm that author.

* acknowledgments *

Thank you to James Sturm for believing in this project. Thank you to Seth Fishman for believing in me. Thank you to Connie Hsu for helping me turn these memories into a coherent story, and thanks to everyone at First Second for giving this book a home.

Thank you to my mom, dad, and brothers for all your love and support, and finally, a huge thank you to Dave and Mel for cheering me on through this whole damn book.

* * *

Tillie Walden is a cartoonist and illustrator born in 1996. She is from Austin, Texas. Tillie loves cats, architecture, and going to bed at 8pm every night.

Published by First Second
First Second is an imprint of Roaring Brook Press, a division of Holtzbrinck Publishing Holdings Limited Partnership
175 Fifth Avenue, New York, New York 10010

Library of Congress Control Number: 2016961586

Paperback ISBN: 978-1-62672-940-7
Hardcover ISBN: 978-1-62672-772-4

Excerpt on pages 96–97 from *The Halloween Tree* by Ray Bradbury. Reprinted by permission of Don Congdon Associates, Inc.

Our books may be purchased in bulk for promotional, educational, or business use. Please contact your local bookseller or the Macmillan Corporate and Premium Sales Department at (800) 221-7945 ext. 5442 or by e-mail at MacmillanSpecialMarkets@macmillan.com.

First edition 2017
Book design by Jonathan Bennett and Tillie Walden

Printed in China

10 9 8 7 6 5 4 3 2 1

Inked with Uni and Faber Castell pens, penciled with a Kura Toga mechanical pencil with HB lead. Drawn on Strathmore Wind Power Bristol. Colored with ink wash (colorized later in Photoshop).